Living with Anger

Myra Chave-Jones is a psychotherapist who has devoted her energy and skills to trying to build bridges between Christian understanding and psychological insights. In 1973 she became the founder director of Care and Counsel, a Christian counselling organization. She is the author of several books including the best-selling *Coping with Depression* (Lion). Now officially retired, she lives in Hertfordshire and is still working in private practice.

Myra Chave-Jones

Living with Anger

TRIANGLE

First published 1992

Triangle
SPCK
Holy Trinity Church
Marylebone Road
London NW1 4DU

British Library Cataloguing in Publication Data

A catalogue record for this book is available from
the British Library.

ISBN 0-281-04571 2

Typeset by Inforum Typesetting, Portsmouth

Printed and bound in Great Britain by
BPCC Hazells Ltd
Member of BPCC Ltd

Contents

Preface

I have come across a few people who say that they are never angry. I would like to give such people a challenge, especially if they are of a non-technical turn of mind. Get yourself commissioned to produce a manuscript by a not-too-far distant deadline and buy a word processor as an aid to producing this manuscript. (This word processor will come with a lengthy, detailed and complicated instruction manual, which will take for ever to read through and which like a dictionary, when you look up a straightforward word, will refer you to another one at the far end of the book.) Try to teach yourself to use this monster which is implacably uncompromising and knows no language but its own. Then press the wrong button just once, and lose hours of work and sweat in a trice. I guarantee you an excellent 'hands-on' experience of anger!

I owe a tremendous debt of gratitude to Frank Kay who was always ready, at all sorts of unsocial hours and in all kinds of emergencies, to come to my aid as I wrestled with my monster. I am also grateful to my long-suffering friends who must now be relieved that they will no longer be bombarded by my questions. I would like to include Mrs Mary Anker in my thanks. She works in the Probation Service and gave me a great deal of her time; she confirmed for me that the origins of anger are the same, whatever one's experiences.

This book is rooted in my own therapeutic practice. I am grateful to the people who have allowed me into their anger, and in particular to Robert Kirkwood who has entered into and helped me with my own. The examples given, while totally true to life, are not direct portrayals of particular people: rather, they are introduced to represent the many different faces of anger. Anger is a huge subject. In this book we can only skirt round the edges, but at least some important issues are raised for further thought. This is intended as a book for the ordinary person, so I have tried to use theory without jargon. It is also intended for Christians, some of whom have particular difficulties with anger. I hope it will be a help.

Chapter one

Introductions to anger

'Well,' he said, 'I think anger is a fairly pointless activity. It doesn't achieve anything and it seems a waste of time.'
'Don't you ever get angry about anything, then?'
'Oh yes, too often. Ask my wife.'
'So what makes you angry?'
'Oh, drivers who behave like silly fools on the road and people who don't think what they are doing – and are even more stupid than me.'

Well, of course, you do have to keep your cool on the road, don't you? It's no good two people behaving like silly fools. But a good many well-chosen epithets are uttered in anger from behind a well driven steering wheel! We know from experience... .

Harry also thought anger was pointless. He was twelve when he lost his temper completely with another boy at school. This fellow then laid into him and gave him such a hiding that Harry has never shown any outward signs of anger since then. He says he does not even feel it, except for occasional irritations and frustrations. The thought of anger is something which fills him immediately with fear and dislike. He will try to avoid confrontation at all costs and go to great lengths in order not to risk upsetting people, such was the influence of an angry encounter in his early life. Harry is not alone in feelings like this... . He certainly associates anger with total loss of control. He says he has seen much destructiveness because of unbridled fury. Most of us can understand this. We have memories of displays of anger resulting in bruising, certainly emotionally and sometimes physically. Those memories have resulted in fear, hatred and all sorts of unpleasant reactions.

Philippa, a bright, intelligent young woman saw it differently. 'I just seethe,' she said, 'and if someone says something stupid or ignorant about something that touches me deeply, I explode.'

'And how does that affect the other person?'

'Oh, they usually look at me in amazement. You have to push me quite hard before I lose my temper like that. But I do it.'

On the other hand, Anne says: 'I don't have any trouble expressing my anger. If something or someone irritates me, I just let them have it. There's no point in fuming internally. That just makes everything worse. It's not always very pleasant, but it's better out than in.'

Marie was less straightforward. One weekend her well laid plans were completely disorganized by the unexpected arrival of a friend for two days. The work which she had intended to produce for an imminent deadline was thrown into total disarray and she felt helplessly frustrated. She had to be 'nice' to her needy friend but she felt furious inside. So she spent the weekend being 'helpful' and smiling through clenched teeth. She was tight-lipped and brisk: without saying anything directly she managed to make the friend feel thoroughly in the way and guilty for being a burden. Eventually, Marie drove her friend back to her home down the motorway at a speed almost designed to kill them both! Marie hardly recognized that she was *angry* but she was very aware that she felt most uncomfortable.

And we could go on thinking of different ways in which people react to something that arouses their anger. But whatever the reaction, the immediate feeling is varying degrees of disturbance, unpleasantness, woundings and damage. Indeed, we see all around us the devastating results that anger can produce in the lives of individuals and communities.

The three sons of a wealthy farmer had such acrimonious exchanges over his will and property that one brother severed connections with the others. A previously united family was split up in anger and recriminations that rumbled on for many years and down the generations.

A divorced mother's seeping fury and bitterness over her husband's unfaithfulness and subsequent desertion had a profound effect both on her and on her children. All of them picked up the side effects in some way; one had a brush with the law, another developed anorexia nervosa, and one of them had learning difficulties. In a similar way, whole communities can be divided by angry intransigence, lobbying, jealousy and resentment. This is the stuff that wars are made of.

It comes as no surprise, therefore, to read the scriptural injunctions which seem to reinforce the view that anger is unpleasant, disruptive and antisocial. There are statements like 'the anger of man does not work the righteousness of God' (James 1.19)[1]; 'now you must rid yourselves of all such things as these, anger, rage, malice, slander, filthy language from your lips ...' (Colossians 3.8); and we know that anger is included in most of the lists of unacceptable Christian behaviour. Are we, therefore, to label all anger as 'sin'? We are stopped in our tracks when we remember that Jesus Christ himself was angry at times and the Bible makes frequent reference to the anger of God. Are we to conclude that God is allowed to be angry because he must have some righteous cause at heart and that human beings may sometimes be angry acceptably if our cause is also righteous? Who is to decide what is righteous and what is not? And what do we

3

make of the occasions in the Old Testament when God's anger appeared to be amazingly capricious?

We know, however, that much has been achieved through the motivation of anger. At school we learnt of William Wilberforce's sense of angry outrage as he saw and heard of the horrors of the slave trade – defenceless people being snatched from their homes and transported across the seas to America, the West Indies and Britain, in unspeakable conditions. Many died on the journey because of the insanitary state of the ships and the totally inhuman expectations of the shipowners who were plying their diabolical trade for the money involved. We have heard of Elizabeth Fry who did such a herculean task in reforming the terrible conditions in British prisons in the last century. More recently, we have seen the indefatigable efforts of the Greenpeace movement to preserve our planet from extinction through pollution and exploitation. Bob Geldof and other private individuals have been horrified and angry on seeing the plight of hundreds of starving people in Africa and elsewhere and have initiated a massive financial response to alleviate some of the distress. Archbishop Trevor Huddleston has waged a lifelong war against the evils that he saw in the apartheid system, thanks to his outrage at the injustice and cruelty that he witnessed in South Africa.

It begins to look as though there is more to anger than meets the eye. It has such negative possibilities and yet it can achieve much positive good. We obviously need to take a longer look at this strange animal which has the power to divide and unite, to explode, create and to excite, in an attempt to try to discover more about its origins, habitat and lifestyle.

Chapter two

What is anger like?

How would you define anger? Pause for a moment and think what you would say.... . People have a wide variety of ways of understanding anger – as bitterness, rage, hostility, frustration, impotence, annoyance, aggressiveness, loss of control, not caring what happens or who gets hurt, irrationality, coldness and indifference. One dictionary defines anger as 'that which pains or afflicts or the feelings which it produces; trouble, vexation, sorrow; passion, rage, wrath, ire; inflammatory state of any part of the body.' This sounds like an attempt to describe a wide range of experiences.

Anger has many shades of colour, from fleeting irritation to boiling fury; from a slight altercation with a manufacturer about a faulty replacement part, to an expensive law suit which involves strong determination, time and commitment. It also contains many of the muted shades, less easily identifiable, which in a picture form the background against which the stark highlights stand out. Anger in a relationship can be rumbling along fairly unnoticed until, suddenly, there is a furious outburst of some sort, and everyone is amazed.

'Anger', like 'love', seems to be an umbrella word which covers a multitude of attitudes and activities which disturb our equilibrium in an uncomfortable way. Many people equate anger with loss of temper. They are not the same. Anger includes loss of temper, but it is much, much more. We use the words 'anger' and 'temper' interchangeably and so we confuse

5

ourselves. Loss of temper might be thought of as a sneeze when one's real trouble is a cold.

So, although anger may appear to be pointless, a waste of time, and unproductive or even 'sinful', it is an everyday experience which we all know at close quarters. Everyone, everywhere, at some time or another, has experienced anger, though the quantity and the quality may vary. Of course, people are different. Some are like C. S. Lewis's brother, Warnie. According to the biographer A. N. Wilson,

> his irascibility, always a marked feature of his character, was poured into the papers of his diary and no-one escaped except, of course, his beloved Jack. He remembered furiously 'the winter when Joy and her brats burnt the whole of our winter coal ration while we were in Ireland'.[1]

Other people are naturally placid and peace-bringing in temperament, genuinely seeming not to get ruffled about much. No doubt our genes have a good deal to do with this. But be that as it may, we all experience anger from time to time, and it is a familiar occurrence in some form or other. Obviously, anger is a *universal* experience. We can see this all the time in the natural world.

I was watching the sea pounding on the promenade at Eastbourne. The waves were heaving back and forth in constant visible agitation: the water beat on the wall, hurling spray and pebbles indiscriminately in all directions. The sea looked black, restless and menacing, and my friend said to me 'It looks so angry', and later added 'I find it so exciting!'

On another day, I was driving along the M25 motorway towards the setting sun. The evening sky painted a startling picture of fiery fury: great black clouds shot with red and orange in stark shapes and slashes of vermillion. Those vivid and strident colours seemed about to leap out of the heavens. It was their strength that was so impressive, and the constantly changing formations. No 'beauteous evening ... quiet as a nun' today.

We have listened to the wind in some of the recent gales, while it tears up trees, hurls bits of fencing and tiling around, howling and indiscriminate in its apparent and frightening fury.

It is the overpowering strength of these manifestations of nature that makes us refer to 'an angry sea', 'the flaming colours of the sky' or 'the fury of the wind'. It inspires a sense of awe and perhaps fear, and in some people seems to increase the flow of adrenalin! In the same way many of us see anger as an emotional bomb – loud shouting, swearing, red faces, doors banging, tears, abuse, emotional and/or physical violence, separation and broken relationships.

Anger always makes an impact and produces results. The children quieten down and stop their fighting and arguing when mother makes it very clear that she has had enough of it for one day. The furniture firm delivers the wrong chairs after having confused the issue twice already and as a result of our angry protest we may find (perhaps!) that we eventually receive different and better quality goods than we had originally ordered. But when an ineffectual boss loses his temper yet again, the staff despise and ridicule him behind his back. The result of our anger may not always be what we want or expect, but anger always produces a result of some kind.

Other people are affected by our anger, and it also creates a great impact on our own life. It can fill us with tremendous motivation for action, while sometimes making us feel miserable, heavy, isolated and in despair, eating away at our will to do anything. Hidden anger can also do strange things to us which are less obvious and harder to identify than a flaming row. Some

7

of the nicest people can be the most angry! We shall consider this at greater length in chapter 3. Anger is very *powerful*. Perhaps that is one reason why we are rather wary of it. We cannot be angry (even quietly to ourselves) without it having an effect. There is no such thing as anger which does not affect anybody.

We are on dangerous ground when we expose our deep inner heart with its motivation and longings. It is easier to cruise along on an even keel without ever plumbing the depths of fear or scaling the heights we only imagine. That is one great reason why we try to keep our angry feelings out of the way. We may think of it as being noble or Christian, but actually most of us are scared of what we might discover within. Sometimes, when we feel under pressure, we do or say something which takes us by surprise. But then we disown the feelings by saying 'I don't know what came over me' or 'I wasn't myself'. But I certainly wasn't anyone else and the thing that came over me didn't come from outer space. It came from the unexplored region within, making its presence and its power known.

A recent radio programme reported some women as saying that during the menopause or at times of pre-menstrual tension they experienced violent or angry feelings that did not seem to have anything to do with them. True, those feelings may have been to some extent triggered by hormonal changes, but that is not the only reason. Some part of the ammunition of anger was almost certainly lying there waiting for the trigger to be operated. We are often caught unawares by anger. Normally it is so well under control that we do not recognize it as being ours.

Not only do we surprise ourselves when we expose our inner heart: we also risk giving someone else potential 'power' over us and thus, when we open ourselves and are real, we become *vulnerable*. It is a fearsome thing to give up our controls and defences. It feels so much safer to regulate how much of ourselves other people are allowed to see. We run the serious risk of being misunderstood, or worse, rejected. We also run the risk of being known, accepted, loved and comforted. Although we all need urgently to be loved in this way, some of us find it hard to accept. The Velveteen Rabbit, in his pristine suit, has something to say to us here.

'The Velveteen Rabbit' is the title of a lovely story by Marjorie Williams. An extract from it goes like this:

> The Skin Horse had lived longer in the nursery than any of the others. He was so old that his brown coat was bald in patches and showed the scars underneath, and most of the hairs in his tail had been pulled out to string bead necklaces. He was wise, for he had seen a long succession of mechanical toys arrive to boast and swagger, and by-and-by break their mainsprings and pass away, and he knew that they were only toys, and would never turn into anything else. For nursery magic is very strange and wonderful, and only those playthings that are old and wise and experienced like the Skin Horse understand all about it.
> 'What is REAL?' asked the Rabbit one day, when they were lying side by side near the nursery fender, before Nana came to tidy the room. 'Does it mean having things that buzz inside you and a stick-out handle?'
> 'Real isn't how you are made,' said the Skin Horse. 'It's a thing that happens to you. When a child loves you for a long, long time, not just to play with, but really loves you, then you become real.'
> 'Does it hurt?' asked the Rabbit.
> 'Sometimes,' said the Skin Horse, for he was always truthful. 'When you are Real you don't mind being hurt.'

'Does it happen all at once, like being wound up,' he asked, 'or bit by bit?'

'It doesn't happen all at once,' said the Skin Horse. 'You become. It takes a long time. That's why it doesn't often happen to people who break easily, or who have sharp edges or who have to be kept carefully. Generally, by the time you are real, most of your hair has been loved off, and your eyes drop out and you get loose in the joints and very shabby. But these things don't matter at all, except to people who don't understand.'

'I suppose you are Real?' said the Rabbit. And then he wished he had not said it, for he thought the Skin Horse might be sensitive; but the Skin Horse only smiled.

'The Boy's Uncle made me Real,' he said. 'That was a great many years ago; but once you are real you cannot become unreal again.'

The Rabbit sighed. He thought it would be a long time before this magic called Real happened to him. He longed to become Real, to know what it felt like; and yet the idea of growing shabby and losing his eyes and whiskers was rather sad. He wished that he could become it without all these uncomfortable things happening to him.'[2]

Does it sound strange to say that the ability to be angry is one of our most *valuable* assets? Like love, it is an expression of feeling which comes from the deepest recesses of our inner personality. When we are really roused, we say things that we feel within ourselves to be true. They may not be strictly accurate factually, but that is another matter. We have 'fire in our belly'. In our moments of passion, we declare in reckless abandon the urges and yearnings of our heart, be it in love, pain, or in anger. We say it as it is, without dressing it up. There is a deep intensity, an inner truth, an urgency that is often missing in the sieved rationality of normal life.

In a recent interview on BBC Radio 4, Paul Johnson, the well-known journalist, was 'In the Psychiatrist's Chair'. He said to Professor Anthony Clare, 'People are not afraid of anger, but they are afraid of the irrationality that goes with it.' That fear of irrationality prevents us from trusting our own deep inner truth. So the passion and the urgency subsides, and then our inner truth becomes squashed down resulting in statements like – 'it doesn't matter', 'forget it', 'what's the point?' Then, we are prepared to go along with less-than-the-truth for the sake of convenience, ease and comfort. And thus it happens that for a great deal of our lives we do not know our inner selves – the inner place where we live – and are afraid to let it surface lest we, ourselves, should be alarmed and shocked and lest we should think that other people will become disillusioned with us. Passion is dynamite!

In the minds of Christians the word 'passion' is linked with suffering. If we think of Gethsemane, it is not hard to see there some deep *passionate* conversations between Jesus and his Father, described graphically as 'sweating great drops of blood'. At the cross of Calvary, too, we hear that strange and profound cry from him: 'My God, why have you forsaken me?' Here was total vulnerability: no situation for wearing masks of rationality or playing games of propriety. Jesus was being utterly true to himself and the intensity of his deepest feelings. This little glimpse around the edges of his 'passion' gives us a small notion both of the strength of his love for us and of his capacity for anger against the sin of the world, which deforms and destroys God's image in his creation.

There are probably only two emotions experienced by

human beings which hold within them such tremendous potential. They are *love* and *anger*. Imagine the things that people do for love. Think of the profound influence that love has on our own lives. It would be so much more pleasant to sit back and read a book about love; and easier too, because hundreds of books have been written about it and comparatively few on anger. But wait! Love is not just sweetness and light. It too has an explosive quality. It can be very painful and disturbing as well as idyllic. It has the power to change things, divide, unite, explode, create and excite. Love and anger seem strangely similar in many ways. Anger can be just as powerful as love.

'The person who is never angry is not fully a person,' says Dr Rubin, an erstwhile president of the American Association of Psychoanalysts:

> I believe that you feel either all your feelings or none at all. You cannot select which feelings you will feel and which you won't... . Negate anger and you must also negate love ... . Anger and love and the feeling of both do not operate in separate compartments or in separate people. We cannot reject one and hope to experience the other.

Anger, then, is an emotion that comes from our inner depths. It is a universal emotion that everybody knows something about. But it can often be so disturbing that we feel afraid of its power. The intensity of it sometimes makes us say and do things that we would not think of saying or doing in cold blood. We do not like to admit to the inner reality that suddenly becomes exposed. We feel vulnerable and at risk of criticism from ourselves and from other people. All these factors make us shy away from anger. We don't know how to handle it. It is so uncomfortable that we form a generalized impression that anger is wrong and something to be avoided.

But actually, our anger can be a potential friend. It can show us more about ourselves when we consider what sort of things make us angry and how we react when we are roused. These deep feelings come from the centre of our being and are very similar to the feelings of love which come from the same source. This sense of passion is the stuff of which life is made. Without it we are tidy and convenient but also anaemic and sterile. Anger does not seem to be something which God is afraid of.

Chapter three

Anger seen and unseen

There is an intricate interplay between the body and the psyche over the experience of anger. It is impossible to divide or analyse each component part. We can be sure only that human beings act as a whole unit, body, mind and spirit together, and that it is impossible to experience something profoundly in one area without the others being affected simultaneously. We were created to respond as one integrated unit, not as separate but connected parts. The physical reactions to anger are familiar to us all – the churning stomach, the thumping heart, the sweating palms, the heightened colour. In an animal the process seems to be relatively straightforward. A cat's fur will stand on end and its back will arch when it sees a dog approaching; and if the dog gets too near the cat will spit. First of all the cat has *seen* the dog. The cat *knows* from experience that dogs often chase cats and so it sees itself as being under threat – rightly or wrongly. Its defensive mechanisms come into play. We could say that the cat '*feels* angry'.

Many of us know that we feel much more 'scratchy' when we are tired and hungry – when our blood sugar is low. Give us something to eat and we are much more reasonable. A baby cries automatically when it is hungry; most children are more argumentative and unco-operative just before mealtimes.

When anger is aroused there is an increase in the pulse rate and blood pressure, together with an increase in the peripheral circulation of blood and a rise in the level of blood glucose. The rate of breathing is accelerated and the muscles of the limbs and trunk become more tensely contracted and less liable to fatigue. At the same time, blood is directed to the brain from the internal organs of the body; digestion and movement of intestines ceases, although the flow of acid and the digestive juices tends to be increased. So if we eat when we are angry we may expect indigestion! During anger, there is also some loss of sensory perception so that men who are fighting can sustain quite severe injuries without being aware of them.

The purpose of all this is to prepare the whole body for fight or flight – the two alternatives for self-preservation in the face of something that is perceived as frustration or threat. The brain releases chemicals which react on the glands through the body. The net result is an increase in adrenalin and other substances which, once in circulation, further stimulate the brain. So we get a chain reaction. The response to anger is inevitably longer than the initial stimulus. It takes a while to 'go off the boil', both physically and emotionally.

Sometimes there is no appropriate outlet for all these physiological and emotional changes of body and mind. They have nowhere to discharge themselves and then return to the normal resting state. In that case, the body's total response to anger is left in suspension. That is one significant factor which contributes to such physical problems as gastric ulcers, hypertension, asthma, eczema and 'angry rashes', tension headaches, migraine, arthritis, genito-urinary problems, colitis and 'irritable bowel syndrome', angina, thrombosis and sundry other ills. Of course, not all sufferers from these conditions are necessarily angry people, and not all angry people suffer from one of the associated illnesses. Genetic and other factors are involved. But it is a well-established fact that emotional and physical dysfunction go hand in hand.

Anger is simply an automatic defensive reaction and therefore morally neutral. In itself it is just energy and no more culpable than other instinctual reactions such as hunger for food and love or sex, or ambition. However, like these other instinctual reactions, it has the potential for disaster if it is not handled adequately. It is because we so often see these instincts expressed destructively that we come to regard them as wrong in themselves. They are not; it is what we do with them that determines whether or not they are destructive.

Anger can have disastrous effects if it is expressed whenever and however we feel like so doing. Such indiscriminate explosions rarely solve anything at the time although they may make us feel, superficially, that we have got something out of our system. That sense of relief is probably the release of the accumulating physical reactions. Punching pillows, furious digging in the garden, hacking down the bushes or any other vigorous activity may have the same effect in that it reduces the physical stress, but does not address the basic problem of how to deal with the cause of the trouble. It is like opening our internal windows to let out the unpleasant smell instead of removing the rotting food. Because of the sense of relief that this sort of *ventilation* of our feelings brings it can become an end in itself; but the basic problem will remain. Moreover, such outbursts can become addictive, like alcohol, in that they bring temporary relief, and certainly gain attention.

Lesley was not made of 'grin and bear it' material. It was obvious for everyone to see how exceedingly angry she was for most of the time. She ventilated her feelings at the slightest provocation. She was invited to a Christmas lunch which had been laid on by a local church. She sat at the empty table indicated by the person who had taken her, and began to settle, when someone came up and asked if she would mind very much moving because that particular table was reserved for another party of people. Lesley was livid. She heaved herself up noisily, tossed her dishevelled hair and flounced off to another empty table as far away from the others as she could get, saying 'I've had enough of this: I'm not taking any more!' Everyone was speechless with embarrassed astonishment. The outburst seemed to be out of all proportion to the provocation. But not to Lesley. This was the story of her life; always in everyone's way, always being pushed around, no one ever staying with her for long. It was always the same, and this small incident was a stark repeat of how her whole life seemed to be. She expressed her resentment loudly and clearly.

Lesley was an intelligent girl and had done well at school without too much effort. Her brothers were both professional people and she could have pursued her own nursing career had she not chosen to give it up for marriage because she was pregnant. Her two children were now six and three respectively, and 'drove her mad' with all their demands. Her husband had walked out for another woman before the younger child was born, leaving her with 'all this trouble'.

The house in which she lived mirrored her attitude to herself. It was a potentially pretty little terraced house with attractive windows and a small front garden which had once been cared for. Inside, the mess, junk and filth were everywhere. Obviously, no attempt was ever made to do anything but survive. The children looked like waifs; the cat and the great black, smelly dog seemed to dominate the place which exuded bleakness and a total lack of interest; more than that, there seemed to be a deliberate sense of destruction by neglect.

It was true that no one ever stayed long with Lesley. Her behaviour was the self-fulfilling prophecy. She was like a red-hot iron, so naturally people dropped her quite soon. And yet in the angry heat there was a strong whiff of despair. She was rude and angry all the time, and only people with more than usual perseverance would tolerate her. Her social workers were reluctant to visit much and the counsellor to whom they had referred Lesley suddenly announced that she would be changing her job and would be leaving soon. 'Typical!' was Lesley's response. 'Everyone walks out on me. Didn't I tell you?'

She was the eldest child of her parents, but, alas, she was a girl. Perhaps their disappointment was reflected in their choice of her name. She was thirteen months old when the longed-for baby son arrived. Then, two years later, another son was born. Lesley's parents fed, clothed and cared for her, but found her difficult and demanding. They did their best, but could not enter into the anguished rage of this little girl who felt emotionally abandoned by her mother whose presence and smile she needed so much. That 'presence' was not just physical proximity. It was an over-arching sense of being loved, accepted and sustained emotionally. At that stage Lesley did not have the verbal skills with which to express her grief and anger. She could only behave in a non-co-operative way which indicated her feelings. This attitude reinforced the difficulty her parents were experiencing with her, and added to Lesley's perception of their rejection. And so the story went on. As the years passed it turned gradually into an entrenched position. She saw herself as unloved and unwanted, and the rest of the world as a hateful and frustrating place to be in. Her desperate search for love, which resulted in the fiasco of a marriage, was just one more proof for her. No one seemed to care about her longings for love, and in any case she took good care to hide them now, because to love or to be at all vulnerable was too dangerous. That meant the risk of being let down again; so rudeness and anger were 'safe'.

Lesley usually overreacted to stimuli, as she did at the church lunch. This florid show of anger was intended to give the message 'I'm not small and insignificant. You can't treat me like dirt.' Lesley thought she was giving this message to those other people in the church hall who, she felt, were reflecting her parents' attitude. She had seemed to be less significant to her parents than her brothers had been. But this message was really addressed to herself. Her overreaction was enough evidence that she did see herself as very small and insignificant and therefore needing to make a big noise in order to be noticed.

Lesley knew that she was at war with herself and all the world. However, the damage can be just as great when people do not understand or recognize the force of their inner anger. It is perhaps the most destructive factor to personal health and happiness, and in day-to-day relationships. This inner anger, unacknowledged and repressed, means that the person involved is always living in some degree of physical tension, and is quickly offended and easily frustrated emotionally. Neither the body nor the spirit can find real rest. This *hidden anger* is more often hidden from the person concerned than from observers. Facial expression, the general body language, the quality of relationships, and physical symptoms can be clues.

Emily had been the pampered only child of her adoring parents, brought up in an unusually sheltered atmosphere and given every material comfort. They were a devoted threesome. The only apparent trouble was that from time to time Emily's mother would explode in uncontrollable temper. These scenes were terrifying and Emily used to be virtually paralysed with fear. She would creep up to her bedroom and wait there until it seemed safe to emerge. She would conclude that somehow or other it must be her fault and wonder what she could do about it. She felt helpless and, naturally, soon decided that any expressions of any anger were totally destructive and to be avoided at all costs. She buried any resentment she felt about her lonely childhood and the anxious-making behaviour of her mother. She willingly joined the ranks of the people who believe that they, themselves, are never angry. She hid her anger.

In the course of time she married. Emily and Peter were much in love but as they began to settle down together, they, of course, discovered ways in which they irritated each other. When Peter vented his wrath Emily was shocked and afraid, and the childhood memories and feelings of fear and foreboding came flooding back. She retreated into her emotional shell and started to take the high moral ground of condemnation: 'You shouldn't be like that: you should be able to control yourself.' So Peter soon discovered that it was not wise to be honest: the repercussions were too troublesome. He swallowed his annoyance on a regular basis. So there were two of them who 'never had a cross word'! As the years went by, Peter built up a huge amount of accumulated resentment of which Emily was largely unaware. She considered that they had a good marriage: her only complaint was that Peter was not very loving these days. They were, actually, becoming increasingly estranged from one another and in despair they eventually went to seek some outside help. This was difficult for them, and only a last resort. After all, they were Christian people and, therefore, they thought they ought to be able to sort things out without 'dragging outsiders in'. They both believed that anger was very unseemly in a Christian, and that prayer and a bit of effort should be enough. But it did not work.

It was painful in the extreme for Emily and Peter to face separately and together that they had such very angry feelings hidden away. Peter's anger was more readily available to him: they were sitting like a heavy, indigestible lump inside him. Emily had a worse time: she believed herself to be a 'good

21

Christian' and she could not bear to acknowledge the hidden areas that she had been at such pains to exclude from her awareness, even in the everyday things of life. It was hard work for her to be faced with the huge barriers she had erected to defend herself against the anger of which she was so terrified; that her 'morality' was somewhat phoney because it was based on fear; that anger usually carries some message and is not simply bad temper; and that the message needs to be deciphered. As she was able, very slowly and painfully, to look at herself and her lifestyle and become more real and honest, her relationship with Peter began to change. It did not become idyllic; it just meant that they were more able to be open with each other without feeling accused, unloved and criticized.

Angry confrontations are never pleasant or easy. We often feel afraid of other people's reactions to our anger. If we are in possession of our own angry feelings, however, we can be firm without having to shout and be aggressive or threatening. If we are not in possession of ourselves and feel afraid of being overwhelmed by our own internal feelings, the confrontation with someone else's angry feelings will seem to be very threatening. Then, in order to defend ourselves against this fear we may begin to shout or threaten. It is fundamentally important to understand this. *It is not, basically, the fear of other people's anger which frightens me. That can have limited power when I have come to terms with my own angry feelings.* I then feel more or less at home within myself and if someone comes 'battering at the door of my home' I am still safe.

Only if the door of my home is not sound do I have good reason to fear that I am not safe. If the people banging on my door are, in reality, overwhelmingly powerful and alarming, it may be prudent to escape through a back window or take some other avoiding action. If I do not trust my own home to keep me safe, I shall either be trembling inside in terrified paralysis or I shall beat a retreat without any attempt at negotiation, as Emily had always done. In general, other people can have only as much emotional power over me as I am prepared to give them, and that depends on how sound my 'front door' is. By 'sound' I mean 'proven, adequate and enabling'. I do not mean rigid, hard and inflexible.

Valerie had a personal experience of discovering her 'front door' in her own life. She had always been socially correct, pleasant, compliant, giving preference to other people's wishes, uncomplaining and a good girl generally, just as her mother had required. She had always repressed any feelings of injustice or rebellion because she thought her parents would be displeased and upset. After all, you can't bite the hand that feeds you. She thought they knew what was best and right because they were her parents, and parents always know; therefore she must be wrong. Also she had come to think that this sort of 'being good' was required Christian behaviour. But in adult life she had prolonged periods of feeling 'down' and 'weepy' and thought she 'shouldn't be like that'. She was under the impression that this 'lowness' was due to some inadequacy in her Christian life. She thought that she would become more peaceful if she were more 'spiritual', and that then these miserable times would cease. She redoubled her praying and Bible reading but it did not seem to make a lasting difference.

She began to understand, when she herself became a mother, why her parents needed to have such a good daughter. They had their own insecurities and desire to convince their own parents and themselves that they were a success at parenting. Even in adulthood, Valerie still wanted to protect them from any unpleasantness so she rationalized her behaviour on that basis and said that their restricting demands on her were not really their fault. She also wanted to protect herself from any embarrassing interchanges. However, she became increasingly angry about the 'legacy she had been landed with' and her 'straitjacket'. She did not feel as though she herself was a 'real' person and she could not make honest and genuine relationships with other people because she knew she was too anxious to please.

Valerie was increasingly able to recognize that the familiar headache was her angry feelings presenting themselves in a more acceptable guise. She could then acknowledge these feelings, although it was initially easier to say 'I have a headache' than to say 'I am very angry'. She did not always know what she was angry about, but she became more able to explore her feelings and not push them under the carpet, as had been her accustomed habit. She slowly discovered her 'front door' was becoming stronger. She did not have to run away as soon as she sensed someone 'knocking'. Some of her fear and guilt began to disappear and her relationship with her mother became more honest. She could trust herself to disagree or challenge, and to her surprise her mother seemed much less fragile than she had imagined. Another surprise was that she found herself increasingly able to withstand the heavy demands of her own four-year-old daughter without being scared of initiating a temper tantrum. It was not easy, of course. Nor was it sudden. Genuine growth seldom is.

Valerie understood, naturally, that there is absolutely nothing wrong with being a pleasant sort of person. The falseness of this position is revealed only when it does not really work; then there are constant, tell-tale surges of irritation, frustration or depression which do not seem to have a legitimate or proportionate cause and are not being satisfactorily expressed.

When the rough and tumble of family frustrations are dealt with firmly, fairly and sympathetically, everyone is allowed to experience their deep feelings and express them appropriately. Together, the fears, misunderstandings, hurts and injustices and anger can be aired and dealt with openly. The joys and excitements can also be participated in together. Then everything has an added richness and there is a deeper trust.

There are, of course, *two sides to an angry outburst*. We have a double problem here in having to cope simultaneously with the other person's outrage and our own. We are both giving and receiving at the same time. There seem to be several ways of doing this. If we feel we are being attacked we can withdraw physically or emotionally by walking out or refusing to discuss the matter. That way we create deadlock by not receiving what is being said nor giving any opportunity for really meeting with it. Or we can curl up into an emotional ball and become apologetic and conciliatory in the face of accusations, thus trying to avoid being hit again, but not really resolving anything. Or we can launch into a pitched battle and give as much as we get. We may feel better after getting something off our chest or giving someone a piece of our mind, but unless there has been a real meeting of hearts it is likely that not much will have been achieved, and matters may be much worse at the end. Martin Luther said 'anger refreshes all my blood, sharpens my mind and drives away temptation.' That is good, as long as it does the same for the other person. We can easily fall into the habit of 'blowing our top' without consideration of how that may affect other people. That is merely ventilation.

We are not responsible for the way other people express their anger. The most useful thing we can do then, is to try to hear and receive what the anger is really saying. There is often a message below the actual words. The angry wife who is infuriated by her husband's late homecoming yet again, may actually be saying something about feeling deeply insecure and unloved.

Other people do not make us angry. They only activate some dynamic that is already operating within us. Just think how apparently irrational we are! One person's behaviour can amuse us, but if someone else does precisely the same thing we do not find it at all funny, just irritating. Some factor within us that we have not identified and recognized becomes activated and we react with annoyance.

We are responsible, however, for our own reactions. By either withdrawing or cringing or entering into a slanging match we simply perpetuate the anger. By going onto the defensive we may defuse the immediate situation, but only until next time. We can only hope to face someone else's angry feelings when we can accept and handle our own inner angry feelings constructively. If we can tolerate and understand them, we are in a better position to contain other people's outbursts. But if we are at sixes and sevens inside we have little hope of being able to be calm in the face of an attack from outside.

How can we come to terms with our own inner anger? We shall consider that in later chapters but the important point at the moment is that *we are in no position to face the anger of other people until our own has its proper place in our inner economy* — not too little and not too much. That is easier said than done!

To sum up, anger affects us through and through. Our body always reacts to the feelings. Sometimes we only become aware that we are angry because of these physical reactions. People express their deep anger in different ways. Some seem eaten up with it and explode on, apparently, little provocation, though they do not see the provocation as 'little'. Others hide their anger under a 'nice' exterior, but it eats away at them just the same, though less obviously.

It is this inner anger, when it is not dealt with, which makes angry confrontations with other people so unproductive or alarming. It is imperative that each one of us recognizes, acknowledges and explores his or her own anger, not blaming other people for it nor denying it. Only when we have done that are we really able to harness anger and use it constructively within relationships and as an aid for personal growth.

Chapter four

Is anger unchristian?

Some people may be taken aback by statements about being 'at ease with one's own angry feelings'. Surely this is not how Christians behave! For the moment, let me respond by saying that Jesus did not seem to be at all inhibited about his angry feelings. He knew very well that his public outburst in the temple at Jerusalem would not endear him to the Pharisees, lawyers and stall-holders when he turned over the tables of the moneychangers! He did not just stand there and tell them to stop. He actually upended their stalls and sent their money flying (Mark 11. 15 – 17). Quite aggressive behaviour! He knew that his action would infuriate them but he was not afraid of their feelings because he was 'at home' with his own.

Jesus is more often thought of in terms of his compassion, gentleness and restraint; but he also knew the whole spectrum of emotions, some of them very passionate and disturbing. Several times in the Gospels we read that Jesus was 'troubled' in his spirit. In such circumstances a lesser man might have started a fight or said nothing; he might have grumbled quietly to his friends or to himself about the desecration of the temple grounds; or tipped up the tables and run off quickly and then kept well out of sight for a while; he might even have rushed round to the temple the next day to ensure that everyone was happy again.

Obviously, there is more to this incident than I have outlined, but the point comes over clearly – that there are occasions when it is very appropriate to be angry, so long as we are in control of the anger and it is not in control of us! The causes and manner of expression of anger, so that it is constructive and not destructive is the area which will be considered in later chapters.

Christians seem to have a particularly difficult problem in their attitudes to anger. Many of us were taught that to express anger in any form was totally unacceptable for a Christian. More than that, we were not even supposed to feel anger. A mature Christian was suppposedly someone who exemplified serenity, quietness and graciousness at all times and especially under provocation – that was evidence of self-control. We were to turn the other cheek and tolerate all manner of injustice and abuse without protest. 'Look at the behaviour of Jesus at the time of his trial and death,' people said. 'Take that as your model.' And then there are all the injunctions of St Paul. In every disapproving list of unchristian behaviour, anger features somewhere near the top. There are just certain occasions when anger is permissible and that is when the cause is 'righteous' or when our feelings are totally altruistic. But the trouble is that most of the time our feelings do not come into either of these categories. We have to admit, sadly, that on the whole Christians do not know how to handle anger and conflict very well and excessive pain is often caused because of this.

Jesus himself is recorded as saying 'You have heard that it was said ... "You shall not kill"... . But I say to you that everyone who is angry with his brother shall be liable to judgment' (Matthew 5.21). The Jesus who experienced and displayed anger openly cannot possibly be saying that all anger is prohibited. Within the context of this teaching Jesus is obviously referring to the bitter destructive anger which is in danger of getting out of control and has murder within its sights. The whole tenor of Jesus' teaching in the Sermon on the Mount is going for the cause rather than the effect.

So what are we to do? We know that Christians have angry reactions just like everyone else. We all get irritated and impatient and sometimes very angry. We feel distressed by the internal discomfort when our equilibrium is ruffled and we cannot always pinpoint the reason. Although we are Christians we are still ordinary human beings with the same basic needs as everyone else Sometimes we forget that, and try to bypass our God-given humanity. Some of us have been very deprived emotionally which has severely affected our emotional blood stream. All these exhortations to goodness may leave us feeling guilty, inadequate and at times hopeless. Our best efforts seem to make only a small impact on a huge problem. This 'Christian' interpretation does not sound very much like good news: it can lead to a state of quiet despair because our relationship with God does not seem to make a radical difference in our lives.

Martin Luther used to be in this state when he lay on his back on his cold stone cell floor for hours, punishing his body for the sins of his soul. He was a very irascible monk and all his penances did nothing to change him. He was in mental torment over his inability to pull himself up by his own bootstraps and meet the required standard. Try as he might, in all urgency and earnestness, he seemed to make no progress in being good enough. And then the truth dawned! He had been reading St Paul's letter to the Christians in Rome and he 'saw' that 'the just shall live by faith' not by good works and personal effort. He saw that God was not the demanding despot that he had always imagined, not the outraged ogre that he had feared. He became aware in his inner self that his whole understanding of God, hitherto, was false and that the church of his day had got the wrong god. He saw that God actually loved him and therefore his sin had been dealt with already. Sin was not the primary issue any more. The primary issue was God's love. This fundamentally different

31

perspective underlay the Protestant Reformation. Martin Luther experienced the great prototype from which all human relationships emerge: 'we love him because he first loved us.' No more battling and struggling to become acceptable. The battling and struggling is about something else.

To portray a Christian as someone in whom there is no anger is a distortion of scriptural teaching. That is not what Jesus was doing at the time of his trial and death, when his silence was deafening in its condemnation, to those who wanted to hear. He was in possession of his own anger, had choices about how to use it, and therefore was not intimidated by the anger of other people. He could have sent for twelve legions of angels to rescue him from the bigotted mob, as he told his disciple Peter, when the soldiers came to arrest him. Jesus also told Pontius Pilate that he could have no power over him unless it had been given to him by God. It was Jesus' actions, not Pilate's, that led to his crucifixion.

The earthly life of Jesus was an angry protest against the diseases and deformities which crippled people's bodies and the egocentricity, cruelty and ignorance which crippled their spirits. He had overthrown the tables of those greedy, self-seeking moneychangers. He was outraged by the offensive hypocricy of the religious teachers, calling them whited sepulchres, foxes, sons of vipers, ravening wolves and children of the devil. Strong stuff! He needed to alert them to their misrepresentation of the character of God. He knew he would rouse them: why else would he have said it? But he was not afraid. He was very angry. (So much for the image of the gentle Jesus, meek and mild!) His attitude revealed the reason for his accusers' anger: the painful gap between what they were and what they liked to think they were. (Nothing much has changed!)

Then there came the time when Jesus himself was subjected

to vindictive injustice as a result of this exposure of the crooked-ness of the religious leaders. But because of his security in his relationship with his Father he could turn the other cheek at that point. That was an incalculably costly and courageous thing to do in a situation where even righteous anger would have been appropriate. He did not have a problem with anger – neither the inability to express it at all nor violent over-expression. His lifeline – his relationship with God the Father – was not threat-ened; he was, so to speak, in a safe place.

We sometimes confuse ourselves by quoting, out of context, sayings like, 'not I, but Christ', as though the 'I' in me must be crossed out and cease to function and the 'Christ' must be super-imposed upon it. Thus anger has to be stifled under an apparent cloak of being good. But what happens to the 'I'? Are we supposed to flagellate it into submission somehow, with varying degrees of success or failure and guilt, and not much genuine joy? Or is the 'Christ' banished to the sidelines and kept for Sundays and public occasions? Here is a dilemma. In either case a part of us is split off and in conflict with the rest. We are trying to operate from two different focal points at the same time – which is a hopeless impossibility.

In his very helpful book *Water into Wine*, Bishop Stephen Verney says in a similar context (when discussing John 12.25: 'He who loves his life will lose it, while the man who hates his life will keep it for eternal life'):

> These words of Jesus can be disastrously misunderstood. He is not calling on men and women to hate themselves. He is telling them to hate the self as it is in this ego-centric world order, where it fails to be the true Self, and is off-target and 'misses the mark'.... . This is the definition of sin, and the ego self as it operates in this ego-centric

world order displays what are known as the deadly sins – pride, jealousy, anger, sloth, avarice, gluttony, lust. These are all healthy aspects of human nature which have 'missed the mark'. There is a proper pride – but it can become perverted, so that a man thinks he is God. There is a constructive jealousy, which, for example, guards the uniqueness of a marriage – but also a destructive jealousy, which eats away at the peace of mind of someone who all his life wants to remain the favourite child. So with other deadly sins, each is a perversion of something potentially good. Anger can unlock in us the energy to choose and act, and laziness can be a healthy love of sitting still and doing nothing. An enjoyment of food and drink, and a delight in owning a bit of land and a well-furnished house, can lead to sharing and hospitality in society. Sexuality can lead men and women into the mystery of love. But all these things 'miss the mark' where the ego rules as a mad dictator, in a world order of other mad dictators. So Jesus says to all who want to follow him 'Hate that self!' Rouse up against that silly little ego-centric psyche all your proper pride and your anger, because it is utterly inadequate to the truth which is opening up before you, and it is blocking you from the joy of being what you truly are... .[1]

'Be angry and do not sin' are the words we often hear, from Paul's letter to the Ephesians:

You were taught, with regard to your former way of life, to put off your old self, which is being corrupted by its deceitful desires; to be made new in the attitude of your minds; and to put on the new self, created like God in true righteousness and holiness. Therefore, each of you

34

must put off falsehood and speak truthfully to his neighbour, for we are all members of one body. *In your anger do not sin*: do not let the sun go down while you are still angry, and do not give the devil a foothold. (Ephesians 4.22–6)

This is Skin Horse stuff! It is about being REAL. It is about knowing ourselves, being honest, needy and vulnerable and spiritual and sometimes angry in the process. It is about personal relationships and their dynamics.

The sin referred to here is not the 'sin' of being angry. Paul is not saying 'Do not be angry'. On the contrary he knew well the positive benefits and motivations of anger and that anger is an indispensible part of a robust life. We recall that anger and love are two sides of one coin and if we lose one we lose the other and are diminished by it. Paul was also well aware that the Jewish Scriptures were full of references to the anger of God as well as to the love of God. He also knew of the times when Jesus had been very angry in the temple and elsewhere. He makes the clear distinction between a state of anger and the obvious destructiveness of relationships and personal wellbeing that misdirected and unresolved anger can produce. This latter was what he was referring to in the lists of unacceptable behaviour against which he often warned his friends (e.g. 'Get rid of all bitterness, rage and anger, brawling and slander, along with every form of malice' (Ephesians 4.31)). Drunkenness, debauchery, and unresolved angry frustrations which turn into bitterness, are all needs and appetites which have become out of hand to the point of destructiveness. But the fact that they have become out of hand does not mean that they are basically illegitimate needs. Paul has just been reminding his readers that they belong to a new family now, and that they are loved and accepted within it, and their

35

love-needs are being heard. Paul is not saying 'do not be angry': neither is he saying 'if you are angry, push it under the carpet quickly, so that no one knows about it'.

What Paul is saying is that any wilful refusal to put the relationship right, any willingness to let ill-feeling go smouldering on, any determined refusal to admit that I may have made some contribution (even unconsciously) to the situation, can be regarded as sin. This is the sin of allowing an angry attitude to settle down into something permanent, even though the anger may not remain at boiling point. Paul quotes the psalmist, 'In your anger do not sin. Do not let the sun go down while you are still angry' (Ephesians 4.26, see also Psalm 37.8). He is not saying 'Do not be angry' but he is saying 'Do not let it hang around: do not rest until it has been resolved', although the ultimate resolution might take much longer than merely the time between now and sunset.

Moreover, Psalm 4 from which Paul was quoting, adds 'when you are on your beds, search your hearts and be silent' (Psalm 4.4). This could be paraphrased as follows: 'When the heat of the moment has died down and you are quieter, ask yourself a few questions and *really* listen to what your heart is telling you – be silent in its presence and listen; don't be argumentative with all sorts of counter justifications.' The actual length of time does not matter so much; the important thing is that the attitudes are in the process of being scrutinized and lived (not hidden away) with a view to my learning more about myself and making more room for holiness or wholeness. The sure thing about anger is that if it is not resolved it will not disappear.

To conclude, anger is a frequent topic in Scripture. It has to be, because anger is so basic to human life. Both Jesus Christ and Paul spoke about it and differentiated between anger which is an agent for good, improves relationships and achieves change, and anger which impoverishes and destroys relationships, takes over and leads to all manner of destruction. It is important for people to recognize and use their anger for constructive ends and not to be afraid of it and push it down channels where it stagnates and poisons. 'Love is not easily angered' (I Corinthians 13.5) does not mean 'love is never angry'. It means that the love of a well-integrated person is not easily thrown off balance.

Chapter five

Children and anger

There are three main factors which determine the way our personality and our inner experience of anger develop:- our first foundational relationships, our genetic inheritance and our early environment. We now come to consider the first of the three.

In the earliest days and months of life we begin to make *deep inner foundational relationships* which fulfil or deny the satisfactions that we all need for a secure and healthy emotional life. We see a bright-eyed, rosy cheeked baby who gazes responsively at the world. In this child's emotional bloodstream is flowing the confidence (born out of gut experience) of his parents' love. He knows it. He cannot explain or define it: there is no need. He just knows assuredly that they are *for* him. He can ask for what he wants: he can protest when he feels thwarted: he can fight and he can love and he knows he is safe. He cannot love in a vacuum. Their love envelopes his whole understanding and expectation, though, of course, that does not mean that every little whim will be gratified at once. That would be indulgence, which is not at all the same thing as love. In response to this general atmosphere of love it will be natural to him to love his parents, to experience love as a norm and embrace his whole world in his love, including other people and himself. He loves because he was first loved by someone else. He will be quietly confident, which is not the same thing as being self-opinionated or argumentative.

39

Bill was describing his new daughter. He had had three days of fatherhood. This crumpled scrap was his firstborn and he was still watching her in amazement. 'But she does have a terrible temper when the milk does not come fast enough.' You can just visualize the frantic, screwed up, screaming infant: clenched hands and feet, red face, and every sinew of this morsel of humanity focused on her need, and her inability to wait. Whether this activity qualifies as 'a terrible temper' is debateable, however! But it looks very intense and conveys the feelings of distress which this little person is experiencing because her needs and expectations are being thwarted.

Very small children want what they want, and that is all there is about it. Factors like patience, consideration, co-operation and understanding, are quite beyond their range of comprehension, and adults can usually accept that. The baby's absolute dependence arouses maximum response from other people. Complete helplessness is an infant's most powerful attribute. Bill's daughter has only to cry and someone will come to investigate what is wrong; to smile, and voices will be raised in ecstasy; even to sleep, and someone will smile admiringly! Not surprisingly, therefore, although this child is externally quite helpless, she soon acquires a great sense of internal power. She will throw her soft toy out of the pram, and naturally, someone will pick it up for her, so that she can throw it out again to repeat her baby feelings of pleasure and power. This is reinforced by the intensity of her own inner feelings – the sublimity after a satisfactory nursing feed with her mother or the overwhelming sense of rage and frustration in response to some unmet need, which was what she seemed to be feeling originally.

The infant's world consists only of herself. She does not differentiate between herself and the mother who cares for her, the blankets which cover her, or the air that she breathes or the milk that she sucks. Initially, it seems as though the baby treats other people as though they were there solely to meet her needs without their having any of their own. She goes to sleep when her needs are satisfied, and those who look after her cease to exist (from her point of view) until her hunger demands that they be revived. However, her carers are not her slaves, and so minor frustrations are bound to arise. Even the smallest child experiences furious rage and expresses it without reservation. It is a powerful experience of total passion with no mitigating life experience. Just because infants are small physically, it does not mean that their emotions are small! The feeling of rage is total and unmodified. Such are the primitive responses of the amoral infant.

In spite of their limitations, babies have several ways of communicating, the most effective of which is by using their voice. They gurgle with pleasure or cry with pain, hunger, boredom, loneliness and with increasing frustration because they have a need which is causing distress and is not being deciphered.

I am never quite sure about that Christmas song that says

The cattle are lowing;
The baby awakes;
But little Lord Jesus
No crying he makes.

That sounds as though crying is an unacceptable form of communication. How else is a child to establish rapport if he wants to make some contact? A child's cry may be a call for help, and a healthy protest which is life-promoting. On the other hand, it may satisfy a wish for destruction, which is twards death, because he feels so utterly and hopelessly frustrated and deprived. When the frustration is greater than he can tolerate, all the world becomes a torture for him and the wish for destruction then takes over. When a child's screams are persistently ignored, he becomes emaciated physically and cut off emotionally. We have been appalled by the extreme and grievous examples of this in pictures of children rendered almost inhuman in Romanian orphanages, banging their heads on the cot rails, standing inert, out of touch with everything, even their own inner misery.

So, right from the start, some degree of anger is a well-known phenomenon. *The hidden seeds of it are lodged deep inside all of us.* The way we handle it, or it handles us, is the unfolding story of our lives, and will determine the depth of the well of anger we carry within us.

In a good situation, parents will anticipate their baby's needs and give him consistently loving, affirming and supportive care, not exposing him to greater frustrations or emotional pains than his very limited experience can tolerate. There will also be a place, within their relationship, where the necessary frustrations and anger can be lived and contained in safety and respect.

The baby's experience of his mother is, initially, entirely encapsulated in her physicality. He is content and comfortable when he can see, smell, taste, touch or hear her nearby. His entire life, physical and emotional, is one with hers because he is not able to differentiate between himself and her, and he is in every sense dependent on her. In her he lives, moves and has his being. But he cannot 'hold' her in his heart if she is absent for any appreciable length of time. He cannot conceive that she may be thinking of him while she is at the hairdresser, the theatre or shopping in the town. If his mother is not in his presence, the very young child imagines that she has left him altogether. This produces an intensity of both fear and furious rage which is terrifying. Many a babysitter will have tried, vainly, to pacify a child who is 'screaming blue murder' in his rage. Nothing will comfort him except the return of his mother – which is longed for by both parties! The basic anguished and furious cry is about

'Why have you forsaken me and broken the relationship which is my lifeline?' – or so it seems to the infant.

All parents know that within a loving relationship real battles take place. There is an inevitable ebb and flow. These battles are very important. They demonstrate that the relationship is not excessively demanding and suffocating; that it is possible to be wrong (or right) and still be loved; that love does not depend on whether or not we deserve it; and that the power of love is greater than the many other powerful emotions. Anger within the parental relationship has to be lived and experienced in the deepening of love.

The physical needs of a child are obvious and very important. The emotional needs are equally obvious to a careful observer, but less well understood. But they are equally important because they are the foundation upon which the child's growing personality will rest.

The love-needs of every human being involve the regular presence of the person we have learnt to trust; someone who can be relied upon to accept and try to understand us without condemning or crushing our vulnerability; someone whose tenderness and firmness is a solid foundation; someone whose presence constitutes a refuge, a safe place to be and an inner nourishment.

It is important to distinguish between 'need' and 'desire'. Our love-needs are essential and basic to healthy emotional growth; but there are infantile 'desires' which we often feel strongly and confuse with 'need'. For instance, a baby may desire to be breastfed for ever, but sooner or later, she will discover that her needs do not coincide with her desires. Those of us who are addicted to chocolate know well that our desires and needs are not the same thing!

For a tiny infant, this safe place has to be an actual physical, known, reliable and consistent presence. As the child grows a bit older she is able to substitute a temporary representation of the 'presence' – a particular, favourite soft toy, for instance. No substitute toy will be quite the same, as no substitute mother will be quite the same. In subsequent months, father and other siblings begin to be included within the child's emotional grasp, but the deep relationship with mother is unique and of special and lasting significance. As we grow older, we are able to carry the 'presence' with us for long periods, because we have been and are being nourished by it internally. We could say that our composure is 'the outward and visible sign of an inward and spiritual grace'. This 'presence' is something which, as the Communion service puts it, we can 'feed on in our hearts with thanksgiving'. In most loving relationships symbolic gestures of 'presence' pass to and fro; things like food (or in Holy Communion bread and wine), flowers, letters, presents, kisses, looks – all representing that special internal awareness.

The adult person with consistent inner anger which is easily triggered, has usually experienced consistent frustration of his or her emotional love-needs in the foundational years of life. This accounts for the flimsy ability to tolerate frustration in adult life. People cannot feel deeply safe if they have not been securely loved and cherished in a way which is comprehensible to them. How often we meet people who never remember their parents telling them that they are loved, never recall sitting on mother's knee, and never really deeply knowing their parents' 'presence' internally. 'My mother was very good to me but I never felt she gave me her heart,' said one young woman. Some of us have had our trust so damaged and shaken in our earliest years that it is very hard to trust in anyone's word or to believe that we are at all lovable. The only safe position for us is when we can control things ourselves. So it is hard to believe that God means what he says when we cannot control him.

Thus, when love seems to be withheld, or when it is conditional on good behaviour or bringing home the prizes, the foundations are shakey. If I am to be loved, I shall have to work hard to deserve it. Can I work hard enough? When is enough enough? What if I reach the required standard but then slip back? So I am never very confident about whether or not I can make the required grade. I'm not even sure what the grade is. There are too many question marks for me ever to feel confident. The inevitable end result of all this is uncertainty: uncertainty about the quality of love and deep uncertainty about myself. Have I got what it takes to be loved? Will that longed-for 'presence' always be available to me? I see some other people who appear to be confident about all that, but I am not one of them. I hear voices on all sides telling me that I must love myself or have good self-esteem. But where do I start? Am I to pretend to the outside world that I am confident and not vulnerable? I do that already, but I'm not sure if the act is very convincing.

We can see the obvious parallel in our invitation to the love of God. He gives us his heart; he takes the initiative; he promises; he performs; he is faithful through thick and thin (though that does not mean he is indulgent); his love does not carry hidden question marks. There are no conditions: it is just there for the taking. Indeed, we are told that unless we become as little children we cannot enter the kingdom of heaven (Matthew 18.3). The little child, by the nature of things, cannot do anything to earn love; she does not reason or analyse it; she just takes it in and allows it to nourish her so that she grows strong. She stays trustfully within her own vulnerability. Only when she gets a bit older and independent do the interminable 'whys' and protests begin! And even then, when a child is in need or vulnerable, she will quickly lapse back into accepting and not questioning.

In the plan of God, parenthood was designed as a reflection of his own creative love. 'Let us make man in our own image, in our likeness' (Genesis 1.26). Far from our having to create a god in our likeness and call him 'father', the situation is reversed. God is the loving parent in whose presence we are safe, though not immune to the slings and arrows of outrageous fortune. In him we live and move and have our being. We love, because he first loved us. But a tiny infant cannot understand about the concept of 'God' who is outside his experience. He understands very well about consistent and loving parents and later on that experience will have become a signpost towards the loving parenthood of God in a new level of consciousness. Human parents have their own personal and emotional difficulties which are often worked out on their children. Not so with God, who is not plagued with imperfections and 'does not change like shifting shadows' (James 1.17).

Alas that the image of God is so spoilt; but undeniable traces still remain. In the spoiling of the image, sometimes love has been changed to anger, and anger's close associate – fear. The way we handle anger in adulthood reflects the way in which it was managed in childhood. Some people try to avoid it at all costs because it was so disapproved of, or felt to be so over-whelming. Others will try to wheedle their way round it by being seductive, because they knew they could deflect their parents' wrath by a little charm. Others will be very placating, resorting to peace offerings in various forms in order to soften the blows. Again, the response can be mechanical – 'Oh, take no notice. I'm like that' – reducing the impact to something like contempt. In all these devices that we use, including lying about the facts, we are re-enacting our childhood experiences of anger within the parental relationship.

Of course, the healthiest of all positions is the ability to be honest with our own feelings; to state them without trying to shift responsibility onto some other cause or manipulating the situation to our advantage. We may have been wronged or we may have caused offence. Either way, if we are confident that we shall be heard fairly and safely, without undue shock or punitive revenge, it is possible to be angry and to face it without manipulatory tactics of any sort. A loving relationship must provide within it a place for hate and anger otherwise there is no safety in the relationship. These testing times within a relationship are very important growth points.

Susan Howatch describes this foundational and potent force of anger in her books, notably *Ultimate Prizes*. She has been unfolding the history of the externally immaculate life of the successful young archdeacon, Neville Aysgarth. He has to unravel his many emotional tangles and in the final dénouement he pours out the mystery of his unhappy relationship with women. He talks about his mother whom he had always thought he worshipped as a heroine.

> In the beginning I was fascinated by my mother ... she was very special ... that was why we had to be kept out of her way. That was when I made up my mind to become very clever and very quiet so that she would want to see more of me ... *all that withheld love was such a prize*[!] ... prizes consisted of winning the attention of people who mattered ... . Those visits to the parlour for the daily kiss, those occasional pats on the head, those rare smiles ... whenever I won a smile I felt fit to burst with pride. Then Father died and everything changed ... no more kisses, no more pats, no more smiles. No more Mother. We weren't even allowed to live with her in the school holidays ... she had become the heroine again, even though

47

she was the villainess, rejecting us after Father's death. I had to keep in with the people who mattered. My true feelings had to be buried, the curtain rung down on the past... . I was always making excuses for her... . My brother thought my behaviour was disgusting ... he no longer cared about winning her love and approval ... and went on his own misogynist's way... . The real truth was that I was happiest when my Mother and I were at a distance from each other: it was easier to sustain the fantasy of devotion... . I used to feel violent emotions towards women when I was growing up... . Up at Oxford, when I lost my virginity, I started to beat the woman up afterwards. That shocked me... . I thought, '*There's* a demon to be locked up'. So for years I drank sparingly and became a clergyman, keeping my demon clamped down under a clerical collar, and I married a wife whom I could put on a pedestal ... I couldn't have harmed her there. Oh, how hard I worked to sew my demon in a straight-jacket so I'd feel safe... . The apparent cause of that final quarrel with my Mother was so trivial... . She made some casual criticism about Grace's choice of curtains for the nursery. Then without warning the demon burst free... . 'What the devil do you know about nurseries? You spent all my childhood keeping out of mine! ...' The verbal violence came first. Words streamed out of me; words I thought I'd never utter, words expressing *all the emotions I'd buried so deep for so long* ...[!] I was actively expressing what I can only describe as an ecstacy, the vilest and blackest of ecstacies ... at that moment I was the demon ... I was inflicting physical, mental and emotional pain on an old woman who loved me. I hit her and hit her ... God only knows what would have happened if Grace had not

48

heard... . I can't describe how terrible I felt when my Mother died in 1941. (*My emphases*)[1]

The author describes in this vivid detail how the archdeacon experienced the inner thrall of this suppressed anger which was so strong that it felt like a demon. He had had it in his 'emotional blood stream' since early childhood when his mother had failed to be 'present' to him. So great was the sense of deprivation and anger in his heart that this 'demon' had, all unwittingly, influenced his career and his two marriages. This ultimate prize for which he had been working so hard, was the spontaneous love of the person who mattered, who would be 'present' to him and provide a 'safe place' to be.

Although we grown-ups are adult in many ways, we all carry 'the child within' whose emotional blood stream will certainly have been affected to a greater or lesser extent by inevitable frustration of love-needs. We live in a suffering world and thus we all carry within the overtones of anguish and rage. There is no such thing as a perfect parent. Some of us are still crying, internally, in healthy protest. Some have almost given up and are crying towards destruction. *This foundational 'presence' is vital to healthy emotional growth.* The old saying that 'The hand that rocks the cradle rules the world' has lost none of its significance, though fashions may have changed.

We have seen that one of the major factors that determines our deep inner experiences of, and reactions to, anger is our first relationships in the early years of life. At that time we are totally dependent but our wants cannot be met as soon as we experience them. So inevitably we encounter trouble, vexation and sorrow to some degree. If the frustrations are consistent and outweigh the satisfactions, that presages a person who will operate on a very short fuse and carry around a well of anger inside. This basic deprivation is usually at the heart of people who are not confident in themselves and find it hard to believe that God or anyone else can love them sincerely, because they have such a low view of themselves.

Chapter six
Growing apart

Following hard on the essential requirement that love-needs should be met goes another urgent requirement. It is the gradual need to struggle for separateness from this all-important mother and acquire an individual identity. The irony is that unless it is safe to be close it will not be safe to be separate.

This striving for separateness involves a great struggle and considerable angry frustration while the small child is discovering his abilities and limits. Frustrations have to be imposed or endured and that gives rise to rage and tears: the 'terrible twos' and the stage when the child has to look at everything with its fingers – exhausting and exasperating for everyone!

The ability of the young child to 'hold' his mother (or whoever is his primary carer) in her absence is very conditional on the quality of the relationship that is growing between them in their interdependence. It may be that, as well as the child deeply needing his mother, she also needs him in some way which may not be fully conscious. Perhaps the child is a sort of husband-replacement, or a status symbol to her, and she may not be fully aware of this. She needs the child to need her and so he may pick this up and become unduly clinging emotionally – and perhaps physically. Such children often find it difficult to sleep, refusing to let their mother out of their bedroom in the evening and waking constantly in the night. These demanding ties of excessive mutual closeness can be a breeding ground for all sorts of frustrations which eventually lead to angry outbursts of one sort or another from both parent and child. They begin in early childhood, but often persist into adulthood. One of the most difficult stages of development for a toddler is the *necessary* experience of separateness from his mother (or the primary carer) from whom he is deriving his foundational experiences of relationship and life.

If a child is thrust prematurely onto a variety of carers, because of the unavailability of his mother, there will inevitably be some confusion in his heart, so that his level of trust, and therefore his ability to love, may be relatively shallow – 'easy come, easy go' – and his ability to tolerate real frustration much less, with frequent outbursts of temper. Because of the shallowness, a certain easy distractibility often conceals the fact that the roots of trust and commitment are not deep.

Temper tantrums are often the result of an inability to articulate frustration and murderous rage (more 'blue murder'). They are usually connected with the child's difficult discovery that he or she is not the centre of the world and that other people and things have their own separate existence. Children's previously helpless dependence has meant that they rule the roost, but now they have to move on to a new phase with its excitements and also its frustrations. 'The hand that rocks the cradle also erects the play-pen', as Dr Anthony Storr has said. Confrontation in varying degrees of seriousness begins to be a part of life, but hopefully, children have had enough experience in their short lives of love-needs being met adequately and consistently in a way that they understand, to enable them to be building up a reservoir of good will. The growing child encounters anger and learns ways of reacting to it.

This scenario is repeated when the adolescent is going through the process again. This older child wants to become a separate person in a wider sense; splendidly independent at times but at other times very dependent and relatively helpless. The uncertainty can create anxiety and fear which sometimes manifests itself in outbursts of desperate anger. This painful experience often involves both parents and adolescent in frustration, anger and murderous rage – 'looks that could kill'. *This struggle between identification with and dependence on parents and, at the same time, the wish to become a separate individual in one's own right, is of basic importance in the emerging personality.* This struggle begins in infancy and continues as life progresses, changing with the changing tides of life. Any serious struggle is painful, involving trouble, vexation and sorrow, as well as satisfactions.

A mature adult will have achieved some sort of balance between dependence and independence; between dependence and interdependence. No one can be totally independent at all times. There are phases (in times of acute sorrow, for instance) when we are appropriately dependent on other people; but those times pass and we regain more of our independence. Sometimes we do the leaning and sometimes we are leaned upon, interdependently. Sometimes we are independent and do not need to lean at all.

If a child does not become separate from, as well as united with, her parents, she will be merely a reflection of their values, attitudes and, perhaps, psycho-pathology. For instance, Emma was a woman in her forties who never managed to sever the emotional umbilical cord. She organized her own family on the same principles as her parents had. Lunch was always at 1.00 pm; everyone had to be there at weekends; the neighbours were regarded as a potential threat to her Christian way of life; her husband and children were expected to give preference to her wishes. In short, the similarity between her own home and her parents' was startling. There was a considerable undercurrent of protest from the individual members of her family, but on the whole she chose to ignore them, regarding them as 'wrong'. Anger was certainly pushed well and truly under the carpet in this family. It had not been allowed in her parents' household, and it would certainly not be tolerated in hers. That is not to say that it did not exist, of course! It just was not admitted or recognized, so it wended its own destructive way until it got really out of hand.

It is bad enough for children to have to endure the ordinary process of separating from their parents emotionally, even if those parents are mature enough to understand and tolerate the process without too much anxiety of their own. But there is no training for parenthood and parents themselves may still be bound by some of their own difficulties, of which they are unaware.

Some parents find it too difficult to oppose their growing children for fear of losing them. They give their children every-thing they demand; they are constantly available to them and arrange their personal lives to suit the wishes of their children. In this case the children are being deprived of someone who they can fight or argue with, oppose and test out. They are, at the same time, failing to learn how to manage anger – a factor that they will have great cause to regret in later life. It is impossible to fight with someone who always gives in, and so the child either becomes 'a spoilt brat' or else becomes very guilty about his wish to break out. This 'guilt' can become paralysing. It can also be very disturbing and can arouse the sense of need to protect the parents from its force. (Valerie in chapter 2 was a perfect example of this.) Parents may appear to be self-sacrificing al-though, actually, they may be meeting their own needs to have compliant children. These parents may easily create in their children, unwittingly, the impression that to stand up to anyone at all is dangerous or wrong. Then the children in their turn begin to disown their own aggressive impulses which are so necessary for their development into rounded adults.

The roots and branches of anger are very much a family affair. We sometimes come across mothers and daughters where identification has persisted into adult life, for instance. This identification has been completely unconscious until the time comes for the daughter to leave her mother's home for marriage. (She may even have found it hard to leave for any other reason, but this one is socially acceptable.) The realization that from henceforth she will be without her mother's close support gives rise to considerable fear, and maybe guilt, at going away. It can even contribute, in a subtle and unconscious way, to difficulties in finding a husband in the first place. Then the daughter will complain that she feels trapped and angry with her parents, or God, or whoever she thinks is denying her this status to which she feels entitled. If she does manage to make some sort of a break, mother and daughter will make every effort to keep in as close contact as possible with frequent phone calls and visits.

Many mothers encourage this unconscious dependence on the part of their children. The mother is treating the daughter as an extension of herself, and not allowing her to be a person in her own right. Mixed in with all this is the daughter's inability to leave her mother. Sons are enmeshed in similar situations too, from time to time. We know the terrible struggles which sometimes ensue when the situation begins to change! In-law rivalry focuses on just this. The necessary attempt to achieve separateness is frequently interpreted as rejection, with all the associated hurt, defensiveness, indignation and anger.

As we have said, one way a child's aggressive feelings may become cut off and isolated from his or her general personality is to have parents who always give in. Another way is the opposite: to have parents who never do so. In that case people may gradually give up the impossible struggle which they know they can never win. Stephen knew about that. His very fragmentary memories of childhood were mostly of his very competent mother who ruled the household with an iron hand in a velvet glove. This lady was a marvellous cook, very hospitable, a pillar of the local church, an organizer of sundry voluntary societies and altogether a very 'worthy' person. Her disapproval was more than Stephen dared risk. He witnessed fearful rows as his older brother was growing into adolescence, and he resolved never to put himself into that risky situation. He was afraid to tell her about his terror of the other boys at school who bullied him a great deal, and he was very sure that she would certainly disapprove of his emerging sexual curiosity and explorations. Stephen's father seemed a shadowy figure who had little real influence. Stephen was trapped in a cage of fear. He dared not displease his (apparently) all-powerful mother; his father seemed to be ineffectual as a counter-balance; and he saw his older brother as a black sheep incurring all sorts of parental wrath and therefore not able to help him.

So what was Stephen to do? He just did as he was told, and did all the things his mother would have approved of, terrified all the time to make decisions of his own and stand by them, lest they should turn out to be 'wrong', and nervously agitated about change of any sort and unknown sitautions. It is easy to see how Stephen was developing into a fragile and inhibited person, because there was, it seemed to him, no way of 'fighting' his mother and making a cry of protest that would be heard accurately, while still being accepted and cherished. Stephen certainly had a problem with anger. His problem was that he was out of touch with it and so could not express it. It manifested itself in ways he could not recognize like physical symptoms.

The greatest terror of all for children is the possibility that their parents will abandon them. They operate on a short life experience and have few reserves on which to draw to help them in times of stress. They are acutely aware of their own helplessness and so the threat of withdrawal of the sustaining presence of their parents is the ultimate disaster. This could be either their physical presence or their goodwill. If either of these disappears, the child's security is fundamentally threatened. 'They don't love me,' he says. 'It must be because I am unlovable and bad.' 'Good' is what parents approve of, and 'bad' is what they do not like. Thus many children grow up under the shadow of fear and learning that 'love' is conditional upon their being 'good'. They cannot express their inevitable rage and frustration about never being sure that they are 'good' enough, because that would be 'bad'.

But what happens to these unacknowledged feelings of anger? One girl of eighteen weighed eighteen stones. When asked what she did with her angry feelings, she said 'I just bottle them up.' Some bottle! Angry feelings do not go away just because they have not been dealt with.

There are, of course, even in the best homes, times when physical separation is inevitable, such as the mother's admission to hospital. However innocent the cause, some emotional impact is inevitable if the child has not yet arrived at the emotional stage where he can tolerate the absence, depending on the length of absence and whether there is a well-known and comfortable mother substitute. That is one of the unavoidable sufferings that exist in life since we do not live in a perfect world.

If angry feelings about separateness, closeness, disagreements and frustrations are included in the general experience of growing up within the family, they can be found to be manageable. They are basic feelings which everyone knows and are fundamental to subsequent development. If they are not included and not regarded appropriately, they become split off into a private compartment of their own. In this private place, these angry feelings acquire unreal attributes of enormous power because they never have a chance to be put to the test. It seems as though any expression of anger must have nuclear capacity to blow everyone to pieces. And one does not experiment with nuclear warheads! Neither does there seem to be a place for discovering that there is some value in anger and that it is not just something to be ignored and despised. So in the family where there is never an opportunity to work out angry feelings fairly, in the rough and tumble of family living, this powerful, passionate part of the inner personality becomes detached from the rest, operating on a different wavelength.

The Skin Horse had had plenty of experience of rough and tumble. He had been beaten and thrown across the room when the boy was cross, and squashed and strangled when the boy was tired or felt in a cuddling mood. Thus, his whiskers, eyes and fur had been loved off, and he was a *real* person!

Much harm is done, inadvertently, by mistaking areas of normal, healthy development in children for selfishness, stubbornness, temper and other unpleasant traits which might justifiably alarm parents. A small child will push her helping mother away and spend ages trying, not very successfully, to put on her own shoes. If a mother is in a hurry this can end up in a fraught situation, but the child is not primarily concerned with the hurry aspect. Her concern is to establish her own necessary independence and boundaries. One three-year-old girl was suddenly admitted to an isolation hospital in a foreign country. When she was discharged, her mother gave her a lovely new doll and a teddy bear. Shortly afterwards, she was found bashing the doll's china head on the floor with the deliberate intention of breaking it: and the teddy was daubed all over with bright red lipstick.

Was this child being wilfully naughty? Was she expressing by her actions, the feelings that she could not express verbally about the brokenness and red wounding that she felt, emotionally, when she was separated from her lifelines for reasons she could not understand, and put in a place where her mother was not allowed to come, and where she could not understand anything that was being said to her? It is important to be able to interpret the signs appropriately. Of course, children are plain naughty at times, but this too can be a necessary attempt to discover how far they can go and establish their limits.

One important aspect of love and safety is that there are some limits. It is also important to understand what is happening and to distinguish between differing situations. These are the occasions when anger is lived, experienced and contained constructively within the family.

An equal amount of harm can be done by interpreting anxious conformity, which is ultimately detrimental to personality development, as 'good behaviour'. One mother always maintained that her sons were very happy and contented children. The truth was that they had learnt by bitter experience that making a fuss was counterproductive: that their mother was not available to them on a personal basis – they were fobbed off with a succession of short-lived nannies while she was out working, playing golf and living her own life. Far from being happy and content they were living lives of quiet despair. Fear is not a basis for a robust life. Feelings of anger can become hidden away and split off because of terror of punishment or abandonment, if, for example, the result of trying to put on shoes, breaking dolls or crying for mother is too traumatic. These angry feelings may give rise to a variety of psychosomatic or neurotic symptoms, because these split-off parts do not just disappear. In later life, many of us struggle with the results of some of these fears, and the fact that we may have been more sinned against than sinning.

Jeremy was just such a person. He was tall, dark and handsome, charming and co-operative in the extreme. Nothing was ever too much trouble for him. Everything he did was accompanied by a huge smile and 'it's a pleasure'. You could ask him to do anything at any time and he would be there, with never a protest or complaint. That was nice for everyone, but the trouble was that in his business commitments he was equally helpful, never saying no or imposing conditions to anything he was asked to do. He took on far more than he could possibly manage himself; the work piled in because he was so obliging, and although he did work hard and conscientiously, he could not get it out again fast enough. Gradually the customers began to complain and some became downright annoyed with his 'dilatory' response to them. They did not know that although he was doing his best, he was actually getting more and more tired for reasons he could not identify except that he was 'under pressure'. He often had a headache which he did not mention. He did not seem to have enough energy to keep abreast of things and as the customers began to be angry he began to be depressed. Things went from bad to worse until, eventually, his boss decided to select him for redundancy. In the worsening economic climate someone had to go, so the sword fell on Jeremy.

Jeremy's trouble has been called 'the problem of chronic niceness'. He could not galvanize his negative feelings into some useful direction. He was unable to protest when people took advantage of his apparent good nature. Underneath his charm and willingness lay a tremendous inability to manage anger and his fear of arousing it in other people. He had terrible memories of his father's formidable irascibility and the grossly unfair way in which the family were treated, and the business failure which resulted indirectly from all this. Jeremy did not want his own life to be like that, but he had never experienced the possibility that angry protest can be healthy if used constructively. His fear was so great that he could only think in his head about being firmer in drawing limits. His feelings interpreted this as being aggress-ive, so he could not actually do it with all his heart. To Jeremy, all anger was dangerous so he split it right out of his conscious life. He was too nice: too easy to manipulate, too compliant, too afraid – and too angry.

The unconscious effort involved in keeping all this hidden anger at bay meant that Jeremy was always physically and men-tally tired. His tiredness meant that he was never really working at full capacity, so it all became a vicious circle. He himself knew only that he was 'under pressure'. It was other people who picked up his hidden anger in the situation because he was, all unawares, transferring it to them.

So we see that as we continue to grow and establish our own identity we encounter a wider range of frustrations. The family within which we experience all this is of vital importance. Hopefully, we learn within the family when anger is appropriate and how to express it constructively; and, more important, we learn that anger is not something we need fear, because it has been contained, experienced and moderated within a loving environment. All this will have a profound effect on how we handle anger in our interpersonal relationships in later years.

Chapter seven

Are we just made like that?

We have seen in Chapter 5 that there are three major factors which cause us to be the sort of people we are, including the ways in which we approach anger. We have considered at length the deep foundational relationships. We now come to the second factor which is the *genetic constitution* which we inherit through our parents.

As long ago as the fifth century BC, Hippocrates, in ancient Greece, had ideas about the relationship between physical constitution and the personality. He formulated a system which divided people into physical types – the melancholic, choleric, phlegmatic and sanguine personalities. His proposition was that human beings, like all creation, were composed of four elements: air, earth, fire and water. The body took them in as food and converted them in the liver to substances (black bile, yellow bile, and phlegm and blood) the 'humours' of which correspond to the original elements. Even today certain types of temperament are often associated with certain body shapes and physiognomy, for example, the tall, angular and cadaverous body shape is likely to belong to an anxious (melancholic) person; the square, bullish type to the person well endowed with choler (anger); the lethargic and flaccid type to the phlegmatic (sluggish) person; and the open, cheerful type to the sanguine (optimistic) person. But this is all a bit primitive and Hippocrates' 'humours' have long since been abandoned as a serious measurement of personality.

A volatile temperament can be inherited but it does not necessarily mean a basically angry disposition. I am told that not much research has been done, in more modern times, on the subject of the genetic constitution of the angry person. But we all know from observation that no two babies are exactly alike. Some have a much greater will to fight for life than others. Undoubtedly, there is some genetic reason why some people are born with a greater inner robustness than others. As we look at our families it is often easy to trace similarities in appearance and temperament. This is due to genetic factors as well as to environmental circumstances.

Behaviour we learn from our environment is the third important factor. We tend to imitate the sort of things we have seen and experienced in our parents and contemporaries and regard them as the norm in our particular culture. In any modern shopping precinct it is possible to see an irritated mother shouting at and slapping a child; not far away we see children tormenting and hitting each other.

The Iraqi leader Saddam Hussein was reared as a street Arab, living on his wits, constantly subjected to anger and violence and with no understanding of compassion or tenderness. For him and others like him, violence and anger are the norm, as learned and observable patterns of behaviour.

A four-year old was walking along the pavement holding his grandmother's hand. Suddenly, she became aware that he was pulling at her arm. 'What's the matter, James?' she asked. 'I don't like those men, Grandma' he said, looking ahead of them at a group of youths in black leather studded jackets with a couple of huge motorbikes. Even this little boy could sense the unease that was being generated. He felt small and vulnerable by contrast with the impression of their power. These 'men' were, in fact, a group of boys who were all on probation for various violent offences. As 'Grandma' was, or had been, the probation officer for most of them, James was not in a lot of danger!

Several of the youths had learned angry behaviour from early childhood and were very conditioned to 'a good clip round the ear 'ole' – or worse – at the slightest provocation. Jason had watched his father beating up his mother on a regular basis; Darren had suffered considerable violence at the hands of his parents or carers; Melv's father was 'inside' for grievous bodily harm. To these youths, to attack someone physically was a natural way to behave. It was not uncommon for them to be totally unaware of their part in an argument, a scene or an act of violence and what led to it. They were also unaware of how frightening they looked when they started to shout or stare or come near. When they saw themselves on a role-play video subsequently they were astonished. One of them said, in fact, 'I'm terrified of people who are angry'!

Many angry people are actually quite fearful, but have never considered what it is they fear. Their very anger is a protection against some unnamed threat which is probably an imagined attack on their fragile self-esteem. Emotionally they have been reared on a wholly inadequate diet so they have developed 'emotional' rickets. (Rickets is a malformation of the bones which occurs when children have an inadequate and unbalanced diet.)

For the people who inspire such apprehension love is an unsafe or unknown experience. Anger is the safe one, and the angrier you are the more likely it is that other people will do what you want. The DSS client who arrives in a temper and acts threateningly will be attended to before the person quietly waiting his turn in the queue. If you create a scene it gives you a good feeling of power and superiority that cannot be obtained in other ways. It legitimizes poor behaviour – 'I wouldn't have done it, but I was really angry at the time'. If you throw your weight about, other people will notice, respect or fear you. It is weak to show love. If you do people take advantage of you, let you down, take you for a mug: then *they* can hurt *you*. Don't show you care; it's better not to care at all.

Anger is not suppressed very much in such people. Their ability to tolerate frustration is extremely low and their fuse very short. In response to their experiences of physical and emotional deprivation they carry deep wells of anger which only need to be touched to run over. The ones who do suppress it are usually depressed, or doing 'out of character' things like shop-lifting or committing offences with sexual overtones. People are often not aware of who it is their well of anger is directed against. Some incident will light their fuse and then any subject is fair game. There was a recent news story about a man in London who shot a policeman dead because his girl friend had given him up. Another man was walking along a river bank and saw a woman who was totally unknown to him. He had just had a row with a man in a pub and was feeling angry, so he attacked this woman because her glasses reminded him of his father whom he hated. He was just taking his brooding anger out on anyone who was near. This is not an unusual situation nor an extreme one.

Other people manifest their anger in quieter ways like missing appointments, persistent lateness, failure to repay small loans or making paper darts and hitting you with them 'by accident' when having a serious interview. Hoax telephone calls come into this category. They like teasing people (an aggressive style of behaviour), especially if these people represent authority. Authority in any form can be a potent reminder of childhood, powerlessness, fear, and of parents who let you down.

The people who want to be powerful as a way of defending themselves are usually motivated by power rather than love. They have had no internal 'safe place' or 'presence' so they use power as a means of ensuring their position and controlling relationships. Trust, mutuality and love are unknown on a personal level.

Attempted suicide is also a very angry gesture. Murder of oneself or other people is anger at its most extreme. Self-mutilation of any sort – tearing at one's nails, hair or clothes – is about expressing frustration and pent up feelings, a nail-biting experience. Drug abuse is also a terrible expression of self-mutilation and bitter anger turned in on oneself.

Women have developed their ability to be violent verbally and emotionally with the 'lashing' tongue, 'biting' sarcasm and dismissive contempt for men or attempts to exclude them from their lifestyle. It is probably natural that men may want to express their anger through physical violence. Their superior physical strength make this comparatively easy. Rape is one of the battle grounds in which men sometimes vent their anger. Research has demonstrated that there are no obvious distinguishing marks about rapists or other serious sex offenders. They are not 'maniacs' or mentally ill nor in the grip of uncontrollable sexual urges. Power and aggressiveness are more usually the main motives for rape, though of course sex does have some relevance in the choice of the nature of the offence. The offender may use verbal threats or physical force but the aim is conquest and power. Victims known to their assailant often fall into this category and have probably had something to do with stimulating that form of anger.

Physical assaults are an expression of anger, rage, contempt and hatred. The man may beat his victim, sexually assault her and force her to submit to or perform acts which are degrading to her. He may use more force than is necessary and involve all parts of the body. He usually approaches his victim by striking her, tearing her clothes and using abusive language. This kind of assault is not about conquest: it is about anger and hatred. Sex is a weapon that he can use to vent his anger and retaliation for perceived humiliations and rejections that he may have suffered at the hands of other women, and primarily, his mother. A much less common form of sexual violence is committed by men who are expressing their furious and sadistic fantasies. Sexual and aggressive arousal go hand in hand in an all-out frenzy. Although these attacks have a high media profile, they are much less common than power and anger rapes. Sex is the vehicle for all these offences, but they are driven by a lust for power and fuelled by angry hatred.

Not surprisingly, people who have grown up in emotionally deprived environments, whatever their social status, find it difficult to make good relationships. The needs of such people are great and their expectations often out of proportion to reality. The frustrations are paramount and anger is an ever-present problem. Marriage, living with someone, or just sex, is often an attempt to meet some of the needs but has little hope of success because the dice is too heavily loaded against a loving relationship. Too much need and power is involved.

What are such people doing with their experience of unloving or absent parents? It seems as though they have internalized them and have become unloving to themselves and everyone else. All the world is against them and has to be related to in terms of an angry power struggle. It is probably only as a helper comes alongside as a substitute mother, in some way, and gives them a different experience that they might be able to grieve about their deprivation and move on to a more constructive way of living. But helping a twenty-five-year-old to see that he is still behaving like an angry two-year-old in certain situations is a long process. It is hard to replace years of deprivation. It is not always apparent that the adult giving long explanations about missing appointments or consistently complaining that 'it's not fair' is the child stamping its foot and saying 'No. I won't. I don't want to. You can't make me. I hate you.'

One deprived person whose emotional needs are never met can begin a cycle of deprivation. That person's children will probably also be deprived, because the person does not have the inner resources of unconditional and generous love to give to a demanding baby; that baby may not be able to give adequate parenting to subsequent children, and thus it will continue. The scenario that we have been considering in Chapters four and five will be dismally accurate if this growing baby lives in his world where great inner frustration and unmet love-needs are the norm. All his relationships will be based on his sense of need. Material and social status has nothing to do with it. This is an emotional condition which can apply to anyone (though it is sometimes more obvious where there is also social deprivation). It sounds something like the sins of the fathers and mothers causing suffering to the children unto the third and fourth generation (Exodus 20.5).

A relationship based mainly on *need* is always at risk. If I need you, I may never be able to show my true feelings or do anything that might distance or irritate you because you may leave me and then I shall be in trouble. If you need me, I may experience you as clinging and cloying and may eventually become exasperated with you. If we both need each other as the basis of the relationship, that works in a fashion, until one or both persons becomes less needy. Then the relationship begins to falter. It is like the situation of two drunks supporting each other: one changes position and they both fall. When the deep inner needs have been met it will be much more possible to establish free relationships of interdependence rather than infantile dependence.

James' grandmother said that none of her clients who had been brought up in a family where there were loving and trustful relationships carried an unresolved well of anger. However, she did tell of one young man who had now become quite changed. Apparently, as he was nearing the end of his period of probation, his probation officer had introduced him to a Bible study group where members had welcomed and nurtured him. He found in them a new 'family' where he felt safe, and he also became a Christian. He was steadily growing and his whole outlook and motivation had become different. His basic human needs were being met and his spiritual life which previously had been non-existent had become alive. He was becoming a whole person.

To sum up, we are all born with potential passion within. Our genes may determine how strong this is. Our nurturing environment determines whether this passion remains a fearsome beast or is harnessed to be a constructive part of our emotional economy. People who are chronologically adult without having had a nurturing environment may still be expressing their angry feelings in a childish temper-tantrum way by verbal, emotional or physical violence.

Chapter eight

Different faces of anger

We all know the physical aspects of anger because we have experienced them, and very unpleasant they can be. The *experiencing* of anger is not the problem because it happens to us automatically, whoever we are and in whatever circumstances, and whether we like it or not. The problem is about the *expression* of these angry feelings.

A clergy wife spoke about her 'jelly feelings'. She meant by this that if someone said something a bit sharply, or if her husband made some slightly derogatory comment about her in public, or if she did not feel quite in control of herself, she would feel 'wobbly'. She never really knew why: it was just how she felt. She did not identify the significance of the physiological reactions. If the offending husband made amorous advances at bedtime on a 'wobbly' day, she would give him a decided cold shoulder. It took years for her to recognize this as anger. Initially she said it was not anger. It did not feel like boiling fury; it felt more like fear. She said she dared not be angry because she was busy trying to project the image of a perfect wife (especially a vicar's wife!) and mother. So she just swallowed her grievances and became more 'pleasant' and 'smiling'. 'I was afraid they would reject me or cut me off, and that people would see me as a failure. I didn't want them to see me as I really am.' Here we are, again, with the difficulty in being real.

Icy fury is much harder to deal with than hot rage. The passion has gone out of the ice, and there is nothing left with which to engage. The angry person is left isolated in this frigid block. Somehow, the ice has to be melted; it will not melt itself. The only likelihood of reconciliation is the gentle warmth from the other person, which will mollify them and enable them to climb down the 'withdrawal tree'. Hopefully, the climber will begin to see that there is no future in withdrawing. That is not the way to handle anger.

Mary had come to life in her relationship with Charles. She had become vibrant, happy and interesting in his 'presence' – not just his physical presence, but the 'holding' of each other that continued between times. The only trouble was that Charles was married. Not surprisingly, therefore, their assignations were limited in time and place. She knew that the circumstances were frustrating, but the benefits so far outweighed the obvious disadvantages that she was prepared to tolerate them. However, the day came, inevitably, when he was unable to keep their appointment or to warn her. Suddenly, the anger which she had been suppressing very successfully about this totally frustrating situation, flared out. She was hurt and furious and stormed around her flat, banging doors, swearing to herself and composing the speech that she would make to him next time she saw him – if she ever did, because she was not going to stand for this sort of thing any longer! But as the day wore on, the heat of her anger became ice cold. She did not feel angry any more. When they next met she gave him a heavy dose of the silent treatment, was untouchable physically and emotionally, and apparently indifferent. She could not make any friendly move towards him and he did not know how to cross the impenetrable barrier. She had climbed up her Withdrawal Tree where she could survey the scene from a lofty distance, and she did not know how to get down. With a part of herself she could sense a very feeble wish to do so but she was encapsulated firmly in her own ice. She thought she was shutting him out because he had hurt her so badly and that she was experiencing her own hurt and pain by herself. Actually, she was shutting herself out of the relationship. There they were, deadlocked and jagged, unable to find a way of handling this pain.

Mary had had a happy home, as far as anyone could judge. Her parents provided for all her physical and material needs, but they, too, were what is called 'as-if' parents, rendering every assistance short of actual help. They were busy people, full of good works and they did not realize about 'being present' to a child. She had food, clothes, toys, friends and books and they had taught her the basics of the Christian faith. What more could anyone want? The fact that she was often rebellious and persistently naughty was a great puzzle to them. Why could she not just conform, like her older siblings? They did not recognize the cry for help because it seemed to be expressed so strangely. They did not understand that Mary had a deep sense of rejection (which her naughtiness reinforced) because her parents were not 'present' to her; they did not give her their heart in a way which made her feel secure that she had it. There was about them a 'you-have-to-be-*good*-to-be-loved' feeling. Even if they had asked her she probably would not have been able to articulate the problem. It was something she could feel in her gut, but could not explain with her brain.

So when the boy friend had offered love and then apparently rejected her, it reverberated all down the wounded passages of her experience – passages that had been so well concealed because of her intellectual competence and extreme busyness. It revived all the buried pain and hurt. Mary was only conscious of her immediate pain as she made the outburst in her flat, and the greatness of it sent her up her tree. It was not unlike her original

73

experience of needing to be close to some much-loved person, and not being able to be safe.

Some well-intentioned friend might have started questioning Mary about the morality of her relationship or even have told her that this attitude was indicative of pride and should be 'repented of'. The chances are that Mary would not have responded very positively to either of these approaches although they may have contained an element of truth. The friend might have been able to identify with the quiet sadness which Mary was feeling, but might have missed all the weight of anger which is so often out of reach when it presents itself as sadness. In this case, the problem was about rejection and hurt, and the defence against further hurt was anger, even though it was an unproductive defence. The superficial manifestations of anger are usually connected with some deep foundational hurt.

Withdrawal, or 'the silent treatment', is a common method of dealing with huge internal threat and pain which results in anger. It feels like a way of protecting everyone from the volcano of fury that is liable to erupt. When the heat goes out of the situation it may feel safer, but it is actually more difficult to manage. The relationship is severed, temporarily or permanently, and nothing can be done to re-establish living interchange. The very thing which is so urgently needed – the loving presence of a comforter – is the very thing which is prevented. A heated matrimonial row can often end up in bed, the passion of anger having moved over into the passion of love or sex. But there is no warm, comforting 'presence' for the 'tree-climber'.

The icy Withdrawal Tree is a well-tried refuge for people who have never had the chance to discover that there are other and more satisfactory ways of engaging in relationships when the situation has become fraught. It is usually a lifelong defence that has been adopted against the angry pain or fear of rejection and loss of love. But usually, tree-climbers are those people who are only aware of the intense pain of being rejected. They are not aware of their deep anger against the people who have apparently rejected them.

Christina Rossetti wrote a poem entitled 'Memory' which describes this state of affairs.

I nursed it in my bosom while it lived,
I hid it in my heart when it was dead.
In joy I sat alone: even so I grieved
Alone, and nothing said.

I shut the door to face the naked truth,
I stood alone – I faced the truth alone,
Stripped bare of self-regard or forms or ruth
Till first and last were shown.

I took the perfect balances and weighed;
No shaking of my hand disturbed the poise;
Weighed, found it wanting: not a word I said,
But silent made my choice.

None know the choice I made; I make it still.
None know the choice I made and broke my heart,
Breaking mine idol: I have braced my will
Once, chosen for once my part.

I broke it at a blow, I laid it cold,
Crushed in my deep heart where it used to live.
My heart dies inch by inch; the time grows old,
Grows old in which I grieve.[1]

Fear and the inability to express our anger are close companions: fear of being punished; fear of losing the respect of someone we love; fear of losing our own self-respect; fear that the whole thing will get out of control. Fear prevents us from being real. Angry feelings can only be expressed constructively when we feel safe: safe within the deep love and esteem of someone else, and safe in our own self-esteem (or with a sound 'front door'). Then we are confident that we shall be accepted whatever may happen and that these disturbing feelings will be contained. When they are expressed in this atmosphere of trust, they are often dispersed or at least reduced to manageable proportions. Perhaps that could be one meaning of 'There is no fear in love. But perfect love drives out fear, because fear has to do with punishment. The man who fears is not made perfect in love' (1 John 4.18). Where there is no trust and love, trouble will ensue.

Our superficial manifestations of anger usually bear some relation to what is going on in our inner world. Henry Drummond has described anger as 'the intermittent fever which speaks *unintermittent disease* within'. It is the occasional bubble escaping to the surface which betrays some rottenness underneath.

I am reminded of Charlotte Brontë's novel *Jane Eyre*.[2] Do you remember how Mr Rochester, so morose and forbidding, lived alone in his mansion, apart from his little daughter, Adele, and sundry servants? Jane eventually came to Thornfield Hall as Adele's governess, in a world far removed from the deprived surroundings in which she had lived hitherto. In the course of time, Mr Rochester fell in love with Jane and asked her, in his own autocratic fashion, to marry him. 'I love you as my own flesh. You – poor and obscure, and small and plain as you are – I entreat you to accept me as a husband'... .

I abbreviate the story, as you can tell – but arrangements proceeded for the marriage between Jane and Mr Rochester. He became softer and much more vulnerable under the powerful influence of love, and Jane blossomed in a way she had never foreseen in her previous life. But from time to time, in this vast house, eerie screamings were to be heard in the distance. Occasionally a hideous spectre made terrifying appearances in the dead of night. Once, 'this female apparition emerged from a closet in Jane's room, tall and large, with thick black hair hanging long down her back, wearing a white, straight garment, whether gown, sheet or shroud was indeterminate. She took Jane's wedding veil from its place, held it up and gazed at it for a long time, and then threw it over her own ghastly head and turned to see herself in the mirror. Her face was savage and discoloured with rolling red eyes. She removed the veil from her head, tore it in two parts and flinging them both on the floor she trampled on them. The apparition then took a candle and thrust it up into Jane's face, extinguishing it under her eyes – and Jane became insensible with terror.' This violent, fearsome creature was Mr Rochester's living, legal wife, now locked up in the attic and attended by one Grace Poole.

Most of the time Mrs Rochester was locked away safely beyond reach, but all unannounced she would suddenly make some devastating sortie into ordinary life. This crazed woman's fury would overpower her keeper, and she would break out into the house below to wreak terror and destruction. She was 'mad' and 'wild', but her appearances always had some relevance to what was going on in the rest of the house. Of course, Mr Rochester knew that she was there and had gone to enormous lengths to conceal her presence, but she could not be contained. The story continues with the nearly successful destruction of Mr Rochester's whole life, emotionally and physically, because this part of his life had never been recognized and engaged with adequately.

Such is inner anger when it is split off into a separate compartment. Our own 'Mrs Rochester' lives in our house (or our emotional blood stream), the source of fluctuating depression, negativeness, pessimism, criticism (the morose Mr Rochester) or undue compliance, ultra-pleasantness, or paralysing fear. Also in our house lives our own Grace Poole whose job it is to look after our angry feelings. Sometimes she is strong, alert, vigilant, and seldom off duty (like Emily in Chapter 3). Sometimes she is lazy, unaware, or just fatigued by the enormity of her task and easily overwhelmed by her horrendous prisoner.

Philip was another person who carried within him his *passive anger*. He had to exist in a fraught emotional atmosphere in his place of work. Personal relationships in the small firm were tangled and, because he was the 'calm' person, the other members of the staff would sometimes unload onto him their frustrations, domestic and industrial. He would absorb their tales endlessly and never come down on one side or the other. He could always see both sides of the case and did his utmost to keep the peace. He could never bear rows and described himself as 'someone who never gets angry'. If it had been a particularly heavy session he would go out and order something especially tasty for his lunch as a sort of compensation for all the hassle. If the worst came to the worst, he would fall back on his Christian faith and say, 'Well, it's all in the hands of God.' All these devices were appropriate in their way but they were really ways of avoiding confrontation. On one celebrated occasion his patience was really tried beyond bearing, and he did confront one of his colleagues. Although he did it gently, the man broke down in tears. 'I despised him,' said Philip. This was the very thing that he despised in himself! It brought back vivid, horrible memories of incidents long past when he had not been able to stand up in the face of head-on confrontation. That was the reason he had avoided it so meticulously.

Raymond was in his late 50s, tall, thick-set, and slow of

78

movement. He complained that his brain seemed to have seized up: he could not concentrate and he had no motivation. He slept badly and often awoke sweating in anxiety. He had no energy and could not get started in the mornings. He felt isolated, miserable and empty inside.

At the main office of his firm there had been the weekly staff meeting but no one had enquired about his small branch office where he was struggling to keep the show on the road. He had hoped someone would have shown a little interest and volunteered a question, but no one did, and he was disappointed and felt rejected. He did not speak up himself because he said he was 'not one for standing up for himself'. He was not an assertive sort of person, he said; that seemed like drawing attention to himself and being selfish. He thought that possibly he suffered from 'excessive humility'. He could no longer do the sales demonstrations which were part of his job. The thought of them filled him with anxiety and fear, though he did not know why, because he had done them successfully in the past. He felt he was just losing his grip. He was, in fact, showing signs of depression.

Raymond had had a varied history of middle management jobs, none of which seemed to have lasted for many years, though he could not account for that. His wife was ten years his junior, an efficient woman who seemed to be impatient with his slowness of thought and action. While he was dithering, she made the decisions.

Raymond did not remember much about his childhood. He thought it was happy. His only clear memory was one occasion when he 'bashed the living daylights' out of something of his brother's with his shoe. But that outburst of fury was untypical. Normally he was compliant and well-behaved. He hated rows. He could not bear to see people really arguing and shouting. It really distressed him and made him feel sick. Sometimes he and his wife had 'squabbles' but if she got upset it would upset him to see her upset, so he always climbed down and said no more about it.

Raymond's trouble was not excessive humility but a well of unexpressed anger and resentment which he could not recognize. He saw only his distress and his fear of arousing other people's anger. At last, this repressed anger got the upper hand and turned against him in depression. Instead of saying to everyone else: 'You are no good; you have let me down' (which is what he really felt), he said to himself: 'I am no good; I have let everyone down' (which is what he also felt). This was the basic message he had given to himself for many years and in an unconscious effort to disprove it and try to win approval for himself he had taken on jobs which were beyond his level of competence. It was as if he had been trying to grow orchids in a British garden in February, when he would have had more success with snowdrops. But his frustration at failing to achieve what was (for him) not possible, and not being able to win the desired approval pushed him further up into the 'spectacular' which he could not achieve – and thence he plummeted into depression. It was a vicious circle which almost had the marks of a temper tantrum.

Raymond had no one to stand by him while he took painful stock of the situation and accepted his limitations. His wife and most of his friends were urging him to try harder, and while he tried he became increasingly afraid and unable. In the end he came to a full stop. His fear of having to do the demonstrations at work highlighted his inner conflict. His fear of arousing other people's anger said something important about his inability to recognize and handle his own. Underneath his bland exterior Raymond was living his life in an atmosphere of destructive anger.

Remembering that anger is energy, it is no surprise that the absence of appropriately felt anger leads to apathy. Most of us know the withdrawn person without sparkle or spirit, who under-achieves at work, socially or in some other sphere. If we look carefully enough we can usually find the anger lurking somewhere deep down in a dark dungeon. The most difficult patients whom a psychiatrist has to try to help are severe examples of this: people who sit motionless and never show anger or react to anything. They have cut themselves right off from feeling and in some ways are an adult version of the Romanian orphans, totally withdrawn and apathetic. The long-stay wards in any psychiatric hospital contain far more people like this than angry, dangerous people who occasionally make news.

Imogen was a competent secretary. She was constantly in and out of the local health centre complaining about a multitude of irritations, aches and pains. This girl denied having any emotional problems but her body was picking them up all the time. Her whole life seemed to be a sort of 'pain' and in the end she was looked on as a 'pain' by the staff of the centre and most of her friends. Never satisfied, critical, demanding and waspish, everyone knew her. One day she was found in her flat, having attempted suicide. She was admitted to the hospital ward and given much attention by consultant psychiatric and other staff. Imogen was depressed, but agitated and angry. She discharged herself prematurely on the grounds that she was not being given adequate care. This episode was repeated once or twice and she succeeded in infecting everyone with her destructive rage. Eventually, having discharged herself after yet another suicide gesture, she went straight to the underground station and threw herself on the electrified line in the path of an oncoming train.

In spite of all the intensive care and attention Imogen had

received, she succeeded in expressing her deadly, destructive anger. She found no place which could contain her volcanic fury and in the end she 'punished' the world in general and herself in particular for the well of anger she had carried within her for years. She left behind a trail of guilt, anger and sorrow which she herself had refused to come to terms with in her violent protestations.

In most cases, suicide is the *ultimate angry* and unforgiving blow. It is the message of murderous rage. It is intended to create the maximum distress and guilt, and to force the survivors to listen – too late.

Anger, then, does not consist primarily (or only) in periodic outbursts of hot and visible fury. Expressions of anger vary and are sometimes difficult to recognize. They give clues about an entrenched attitude to life that can cause people to devise, unconsciously, different ways of minimizing the discomfort. This is a self-defeating exercise in the long run because it does not resolve the cause of anger and only involves a constant repetition of the unproductive ways of trying to cope with it.

Chapter nine

Anger, life and death

Anger within relationships is inevitable as people grow closer together and encounter the rough edges. Nowhere does it become more obvious than in the intimacy and frustrations of *marriage*. There, the individual wills, ideas on lifestyle, and feelings sometimes clash within the small emotional space. Big, angry confrontations often arise from trivial incidents, signifying a backlog of grievances. The way in which the couple deal with the first big confrontation and handle their feelings of anger, will probably determine how they continue to deal with their disagreements. Thus, they establish patterns which become entrenched. Patterns of dealing with frustration which have been acquired in childhood will automatically come into play and it is not easy to change them. The couple may vent their spleen and have a fight in which one is expected to win and feel vindicated, and the other to lose and feel further aggrieved. After the big argument, the couple either advance towards a deeper level of intimacy and personal understanding, or begin to slide towards alienation.

Sometimes the wife will cry with vexation and that makes the husband feel either more angry or a bit mean. It may end the argument temporarily, but it does not resolve it. On the other hand, they may take the 'peace at any price' option, making half-hearted compromises, evading the real issues and both continuing their former line, pushing their real feelings under the carpet. The price of that sort of peace is usually very high in terms of health and happiness. This usually leads to mutual withdrawal from interaction. Emotional warmth and tenderness seems to evaporate and although they 'never have a cross word' the relationship becomes sterile. A persistent state of low-key hostility and resentment has destroyed spontaneous love.

Alternatively, they may try to share their anger constructively. They will respect each other's position and feelings, realizing that while anger is distressing and embarrassing, it is also a reliable guide to some area of living which needs attention. They will certainly not belittle or be dismissive of something which has aroused such strong feelings. This sort of anger is a potential ally not an enemy. The issues will be discussed until they are properly understood and accepted and then appropriate action taken if necessary. It is not a case of winning or losing a battle, getting one's own way and making one's partner change. It is a case of growing in personal and mutual understanding. It is very difficult and very painful and sometimes involves eating large pieces of humble pie, but there is no other way to deepen love and trust and the riches that follow as the process continues.

Helen was wrestling with herself about her anger and she wrote some thoughts in her diary as follows:

July 90.
I just don't feel angry. Yes, I feel heavy, empty and sad inside. I feel quiet and a bit isolated within and wounded. No point in being angry. It won't change anything. I wish I could be. I want to break off this relationship. But I agreed to play this pointless game so I can't blame you. I began to feel faint stirrings of injustice and anger but as soon as I set eyes on you again, it all evaporated instantly. My prepared speech seemed hollow. I left my angry self in the car and couldn't bring it inside the house with me.

I can't be angry. I'm so afraid I might lose you. I want your touch. If I'm angry and you go away I shall have lost everything. It is as though you will not be Prince Charming any more; just an ordinary man – and I'm not sure that I want that. I'd rather have the illusion that you are the ideal, perfect person.

But I suppose that if I could be cross with you and tell you about my frustrations and appetites, we might find a way of living with them, even if they are not met as I hoped. If we could talk about all this – if I trusted you and myself enough – I might discover new ways of being. That might even make me more able to deal with frustrations in the outside world as well – with people I meet in different settings. It feels as though it might be a key to 'unlock' me. I find it so hard to love and hate the same person; I had not thought of that before: I always thought you either loved or hated – but not both together. They seemed mutually contradictory – but of course they are not, now I think more carefully about it. But it feels rather scarey to be angry with someone you need. Maybe that's what's wrong. Maybe if I didn't feel so needy I could be more honest. It feels so dangerous not to be in control of the situation. I fear that I might lose something if I take my hands off and just see what happens between us. As I am writing my thoughts, I'm beginning to see that we could have a calm, cerebral discourse about all this, but what we really need in order to probe our way into greater mutual trust is for us both to *experience* my anger and work it through. I'm not used to doing that. It feels very strange. But I would so like to be free of this crippling fear of losing you and these awful outbursts of misery.

This was an exciting diary. It was honest and searching for a way forward through the very real fears of rejection or separation which anger had signified hitherto for Helen. She was beginning to see that anger is an agent for growth when it can be engaged and not avoided. It means staying with the anger *within* the relationship. It means becoming real, like the Skin Horse but at the cost of losing the immaculate Velveteen Rabbit image. Of course that requires courage. It is so much easier to say nothing, to swallow the anger, to blame the other person, to cover up somehow – with stultifying results. It means *testing* the waters of trust.

Helen's diary contained other wise insights. She realized that by not being free to 'blame' her husband she was protecting him inappropriately. Her efforts to be caring and fair were preventing him from taking his share of the responsibility in the relationship and preventing her from really experiencing how she felt. In protecting him and taking all the blame herself, she was doing neither of them a service. A relationship always consists of two people! Sometimes we forget that and try to control everything ourselves. It is hard just to leave things and see what happens.

Helen was also brave enough to admit that she was trying to perpetuate an illusion because she might not like reality so much. But lasting growth in relationships is not based on illusion!

In these crucial engagements there are three important maxims: (1) commitment to the growth of each partner individually, and the marriage relationship itself; (2) effective communication – making sure that the whole story is told, treated with respect, heard and accepted as being a valid part of the teller; (3) constructive conflict which is prepared to listen fairly and speak honestly, which does not use manipulative tactics, and which is not seeking for victory over the partner. Anger within marriage or any other relationship is the same as anger within the parental relationship. This anger has to be lived and not avoided, and a safe place found for it so that it can be incorporated and eventually defused.

Anger is one of the necessary stages in the process of *bereavement*. It is a form of healthy protest against the hurtful separation that has been experienced. 'That doctor misdiagnosed the condition: I shall sue the hospital' ... 'Those church people call themselves Christians but they never came to visit her' ... 'His boss was a slave-driver; no one could have been expected to work those hours' ... 'I feel so cheated: we were just looking forward to a lovely retirement together.'

Anger is sometimes directed against the deceased person. Rosamunde Pilcher, in *The Shell Seekers*, describes how Doris, an evacuee from the East End of London, reacted to the news that her young soldier husband had been killed in France during the war.

> Doris was immensely brave. She wept, of course, unleashing her grief and rage in a sort of tirade against her young husband, who had been 'such a bloody fool as to go and get himself killed... .'
> 'Don't cry, Doris. You must show the boys how to be brave. Tell them to be proud of their father... .Teach them to be good men, just as he was.'
> 'He wasn't all that good. He was a bloody nuisance sometimes.' The tears receded, and the ghost of a smile showed on Doris's face. 'Coming home drunk from the football; falling into bed with his boots on.'[1]

Anger may also be directed against God for allowing such a disaster. C. S. Lewis experienced just that, after the death of his

87

wife, Joy, which terminated their too few years of marriage. 'God is a very absent help in trouble' he wrote caustically in his diary, making his own bitter paraphrase of Psalm 46.1. In the heat of his grief and anger he protested against 'the Cosmic Sadist'.[2] That is the desperate honesty of unendurable anguish: the anger of someone who has watched the hideousness and indignity of death wreaking its havoc on someone he loved.

Shakespeare describes it in the classic story of Macbeth, as Malcolm and Ross are trying to comfort MacDuff over the wanton murder of his wife and son:

> *Did heaven look on –*
> *And would not take their part?*

Anger is a normal part of the feelings of sorrow, grief, injustice, disappointment and anxiety. The degree of anger depends very much on the circumstances of the death, the quality of the relationship, and whether there has been an adequate goodbye.

Divorce is also a common cause of much bitterness and anger because of the circumstances and as a response to the loss involved and the associated worries. Indeed, the anger involved in divorce can be sorer than in bereavement, if it is felt that there has been betrayal, rejection and deceit. This anger can also be protracted because of financial complications and negotiations about access to children. In one sense, the anger in bereavement can be good unless there is crippling guilt involved: but in divorce there is more likelihood of constant reactivation of trouble, vexation and sorrow. It sometimes happens that the divorce occurs for the very reason that the unmet needs of childhood are still unmet in the marriage. The break up is the result of continued angry frustration.

There are times when we become stuck, harbouring in our hearts some anger which cannot engage with the object of the anger. It may be a parent long *dead* or someone who, though living, has passed right out of our life: a spouse, friend, boss. We are left with smouldering embers which burst into flames if we think about the situation. We may think that there is nothing to be done about this now. We carry within ourselves the hurt inflicted and the angry response, and now it is too late to have a confrontation or make reparation. We may not want to anyway. Our perception of the person whom we regard as 'bad' has settled down inside us and become lodged in a hardened and entrenched position of guilt, blame, anger or alleged indifference. We entertain thoughts about the injustice, the callousness, or the misunderstandings that have been dealt out to us and that leaves no space for any softening of our attitude. We fail to see any contribution, deliberate or by default, that we may have made to the unhappy situation. So now our own hearts have turned 'bad'. In this case there is no genuine grieving for lost opportunities and missed relationship so the anger rumbles on. Sometimes guilt does not feel like anger. 'I feel ashamed that I have not been the daughter I ought to have been' – and the element of anger becomes lost. The question is not asked or answered honestly 'Was he the father that he might have been?' Any mutual responsibility is precluded and there is no room for the anger if one person takes all the guilt.

The undercurrent of that anger with people who are now out of reach is linked with unmet dependency needs for approval, love, recognition, or something similar. Not until we ourselves have moved on in our own emotional growth and have genuinely stopped feeling that they owe us something can we let go of our anger. We no longer need their approval.

Anger disguises itself in many ways which makes it hard to identify. We don't like its true face – it seems unacceptable – so it gets converted into other things and hides behind them.

Depression is one of its disguises. Depression has several causes. The one that is, perhaps, the hardest to live with is that apparently irrational sense of gloom and desolation which seem to have no external cause, no outward circumstances to warrant such despairing feelings. This is usually traceable back to unmet emotional needs in childhood, the time when the child is very dependent on its parents' love and affirmation. The experience of that love is deficient in some way, but the child dare not protest angrily to its parents because the atmosphere of trust is unsafe. The child thinks that if she is naughty in this way, what little love is available might be withdrawn, and then where would she be? So what happens to her feelings of fury? For sure, they do not go away. They are pushed deep inside herself so that she stops recognizing them for what they are. Instead of being *aggressively* able to say, 'I am angry with you ... you are no good ... you don't love me' and so on, the message is turned *passively* inside out to read, 'I am no good ... I am not worth anything ... I can't do anything ... I am unlovable' and so on. Unless this situation is repaired in some way, by a new and safe relationship, this child will carry the depressive low self-esteem into adult life where it will make its miserable presence felt from time to time.

Margaret was caught in this trap. She was a warm, jolly, motherly person, always smiling and happy. Suddenly, in her mid-40s she slid into a clinical depression. Something to do with her hormones, possibly, she told herself. It is always more comfortable to have a physical diagnosis. But this was not the whole story. Margaret's mother had languished in her bed of unspecified sickness during much of Margaret's childhood and a housekeeper had looked after the two girls. The housekeeper's own daughter lived there, and Margaret, being slightly older than the other two became the odd one out and the one who was expected to do many errands and jobs. She felt all this keenly but there was no one to whom she could protest because her mother was, to all intents and purposes, non-functioning, and the housekeeper was too harsh. Margaret was desperate for love and took to stealing and habitual lying, hoping, secretly, that she would be found out and thereby gain some sort of attention. It was really a cry for help in a healthy way. But the friendly souls in the village put two and two together and made five. They said nothing. Margaret was ten when she was sent off to boarding school and effectively sent out of the way.

During her absence Margaret's mother made a miraculous recovery and the housekeeper was no longer needed. Later, and as soon as possible, Margaret married a local village lad to establish her own home where she could be loved in her own right. They had six years together and a little daughter. Then her father died and within a month, Margaret's second daughter was born and grandmother at once moved in and virtually took over the new baby 'as a replacement for your father'. So, once again, Margaret was playing the second fiddle role. Twenty years later, with grandmother still in residence and having alienated the second daughter, Margaret had some unpleasant experiences with the management of the local playgroup that she used to run. This precipitated the depression. It is true that the playgroup incident was disappointing and hurtful but it did not warrant a reaction of this magnitude.

Margaret had always been aware of the poor relationship between her mother and herself and in the course of therapy she began to be horribly aware of the 'savage' anger within her, literally murderous rage: 'I could kill her'. A lifetime of unacknowledged frustration, fury and dissatisfaction sat beneath that smiling face which could not deal with anger openly but turned it in on itself. Her mother was now an invalid again, so what could Margaret do? She felt trapped.

She began to see more clearly that in this relationship with her mother there was much mutual *dependence* which had locked them together for so long. Within the dependence lay a great deal of hostility: the 'innocent' hostility of the person who expects to be waited on, and the unrecognized hostility of the person who cannot bring herself to arrange alternative accommodation for the old lady but continues to 'care' for her with such resentment and anger. All sorts of reasons were forthcoming about why she could not 'turn her mother out after all these years'. Some of the reasons were valid, and some seemed to be Christian, but Margaret had to recognize her heavily concealed basic wish to do so and yet her fear of doing it. She had to come to terms with this before she could make a *free* choice about what the future alternatives should be. There was too much closeness here; not the closeness of love but the closeness of dependent need (see Chapter 6).

The constant care of a helpless demanding baby (a small one as well as a big one) sometimes evokes a similar anger. As we know, it can boil right over into terrible battering episodes if the deprived child within the mother-figure is overcome by the demanding needs of the baby-figure. The tired, harrassed, carer, who may not have enough money or enough emotional or physical support herself and may be crying out for someone to love and help *her*, suddenly lashes out in a fit of baby – or granny – bashing.

Mrs Smith was a foster mother employed by a local authority. She was one of the best on their books and had been used very successfully for years with some quite difficult children. One day she arrived, very puzzled, in the social worker's office bearing a letter she had just received from a parent which was thoroughly unpleasant and full of inaccuracies and unjust accusations.

'What a nerve!' said the social worker. 'Aren't you furious about this?'

'No' said Mrs Smith.

'Well, I would be.'

'No, I don't feel angry. I just feel sad that she should need to write to me like this. But I am not angry.'

A few months later this letter was being discussed again.

'Well, yes. I suppose I am angry, really; it's very unfair. But I just don't know how to be angry.'

Mrs Smith was a genuinely kind woman but she had been in the habit of repressing her own appetites and needs for so long that she was out of touch with her anger and could not find it when some appropriate action was needed. She was not the sort to harbour grudges, but she was resorting to the well known '*more in sorrow than in anger*' device. Sorrow was acceptable, but anger was not.

Bernard was hoping to be elected chairman of the Board of Governors of the prestigious local school. He had been on the board for years and had all the necessary experience and qualifications, he thought. But to his chagrin, his rival, Alan, won a few more votes. Bernard was not angry, of course! He was just sarcastic, critical and unsupportive. He was hardly aware of his angry envy but expressed it by saying 'Rotten job! I wouldn't want it!' There was a third man who could just as easily have been elected. This man was not ambitious nor striving for recognition, so Bernard was not in emotional competition with him. He did not fear rejection and displacement by this man. But he convinced himself that Alan was being aggressive and suspicious of him though he could not see the extent of his own angry feelings. He 'dealt' with them by projecting them onto

Alan, whom he regarded as a rival, thus managing to avoid them.

Audrey was full of *distorted anger*. She was a young woman in her mid-twenties; very slim, attractive, neatly dressed, efficient, undemanding, very softly spoken, and looking quite self-possessed. She would sit quietly in the corner awaiting her turn. She seemed almost, but not quite, too good to be true. She said that she had not had any great traumas in her early years and, therefore, she ought not to have any problems now. She was just being stupid, childish and self-indulgent, making a big fuss about nothing when there were people all around in much greater distress than she. She was never 'pushy' or noisy. She had learnt long ago that if her needs were not going to be met it was better not to have any. She had pulled down the shutters on her appetites and now did not, she thought, really have any. Somehow, to ask outright for what she wanted seemed to be courting rejection. The word 'appetites' had, for her, overtones of greed and excess and did not come into the normal category of health-preserving urges like hunger for food, love, sex, or beauty or exercise. But inside, Audrey was not docile and silent: she felt very desperate from time to time, and her efforts at self-flagellation did not ease that desperation. She was busy mis-applying what she thought was a Christian exhortation to deny herself. This reinforced her self-condemnation as she treated herself internally with considerable harshness. She seemed to know nothing at all, in her experience, of the freely available Christian promise of 'rivers of living water' flowing from her inner self. She seemed to be living more on the level of a refugee, like the Kurdish people, trying desperately to survive in impossible conditions, struggling barefoot in mud and freezing temperatures in mountains that offered no shelter or food.

Audrey had spent years in this state with no 'presence' or safe place to be. She had reached the point of hating herself. It was easy for her to believe the negative things that people said about her but if someone reached out with a gentle or affirming remark, she could not believe that they meant it. She could not see anything good or lovable about herself on any level, and life was often almost intolerable for her. And all this despairing struggle was going on underneath a quiet, well-behaved, 'Christian' exterior.

After a time in a safe environment, Audrey was able to see how angry she was: how this undemanding façade was covering a huge, silent, roaring anger against 'circumstances' in her past. These circumstances were a mother who 'did not give me her heart'. She gave food, clothes, education and plenty of externals, but did not see the loneliness of her only child: did not understand Audrey's grief when she went out evening after evening, leaving Audrey with the father of whom she was a bit afraid; did not realize Audrey's anguish when she witnessed violent parental quarrels; did not see that Audrey's lack of confidence was due to feelings that were completely stifled for fear of causing trouble. Because the child had no one with whom to share them she had to bury them. Audrey's mother gave her every assistance short of actual help! Thus, Audrey came to believe that she had no feelings or appetites and that it was bad to have them. But Audrey was not so passive as all that. She was aware of the intense inner turmoil which turned out to be extreme anger about these 'circumstances'.

However, she found it much more difficult to recognize the angry attack she made on other people, when she metaphorically knocked out of their hand the gentle gift of affirmation. We do not make consistent and serious attacks on other people for fun: we do it because we are angry, though not necessarily with them. Audrey was angry with herself for being what she was. She was unable to 'mother' herself because she had not been mothered adequately. She could not permit herself to be needy or make allowances for herself and listen to her own appetites. Every little internal cry was silenced at once and regarded as potential wickedness, without giving it a chance to be deciphered properly. She was angry with other people because they represented the mother who had not recognized and therefore had effectively denied her basic human needs.

This deprived and infected blood stream had run together with certain 'Christian' teachings in the negative way that fitted in with her emotional predisposition. She had preconceived ideas about how a Christian 'ought' to behave; standards of near-perfection that she tried exhaustingly to achieve, leaving herself feeling a guilty failure; the emotional conviction that a rather forbidding and powerful God's love for her was conditional on whether or not she was worthy of it – though intellectually she knew this was not true. The general attitude of trying not to be a nuisance at home had crept into her thoughts about Christian teaching and she had the utmost difficulty in letting go of her need to be good in order to be loved. It was as she began to experience a safe place where she could explore some of her fears and intense anger which had become distorted into 'goodness' that she became more able to relax and life became less of a burden. She also began to be able to relate to God in a new way with something more like pleasure than burdensome duty, and to be less harsh with herself.

To conclude, this vital experience of anger is present with us in our living relationships and most of life's experiences. The more intimate the relationship the more likely we are to encounter our anger. It is part of the passion of living. We can embrace it to learn more about the way we function and thus deepen our relationships or we can try to sidestep it in some way, to our cost.

Chapter ten

Dealing with anger

If we look at things superficially, and ignore, for the moment, the underground river, we might assume that, given enough motivation, we can unlearn the behaviour we have adopted. It may be helpful here to consider some of the techniques which people can use to help themselves.

There is usually a build-up in the process of anger, though people are often unaware of it and they just 'go mad' or 'see red'. What are the flashpoints? Was it an insult? Was it that someone was staring or shouting? At what stage does an increased heart beat, rate of breathing or a feeling of tension begin. The physical reactions must be activated and it is easy to miss those warning signs which indicate that an outburst or crisis is not far off. Before we can do anything, like shouting or hitting or throwing a plate, a message goes from the brain so that the nerves and muscles are geared into action. In long-standing behaviour patterns the paths to and from the brain will have become well trodden so that the reaction is almost automatic. The path has to be broken up by different patterns.

There are certain trigger situations which start the process of anger, such as the person who parks his car in our space, the adolescent who treats the house like a hotel, the person who elbows his way to the counter instead of waiting in the queue, people who spend too long in the bathroom, and so on. They include questions like 'Who do you think you are?' or anything which suggests that we are remotely inferior. There must be some reason why situations and remarks like this trigger such a volume of feeling. Could it be a flashback to childhood frustrations? We need to think carefully about the implications of it. One response could be to block the pathway to the brain by such reactions as 'I'm not going to let a thing like that get to me' or 'I don't want to stoop to that sort of behaviour', or 'I am beginning to recognize here my needy/greedy child'.

You may be familiar with William Blake's lines from 'A Poison Tree':

I was angry with my friend:
I told my wrath; my wrath did end.
I was angry with my foe.
I told it not; my wrath did grow.

And I watered it in fears
Night and morning with my tears;
And I stunned it with smiles
And with soft, deceitful wiles;

And it grew both day and night
Till it bore an apple bright,
And my foe beheld it shine
And he knew that it was mine,

And into my garden stole
When the night had veiled the pole;   (star)
In the morning glad I see
My foe outstretched beneath the tree.[1]

In this poem Blake outlines much that we have been considering. Clearly, 'I' nursed my anger with fears and protected it with all sorts of subtle wiles (such as denying, avoiding, distorting or converting it into other things). It did not go away: on the contrary, I was nursing it into something special which looked good and faultless – on the outside. But my enemy obviously did not trust me because he wanted to steal it from me and so he crept in unawares. Then the real truth about me appeared; I was glad when he got his 'just deserts'. The apple is reminiscent of the fruit in the Garden of Eden which is the timeless symbol of broken relationships, bringing endless trouble, vexation and sorrow. And it all began because I did not share my anger but kept it as a private secret of my own. What was there about this person that made him or her into a foe for me? Or was it something about me?

One of the essentials in the *management of anger* is to recognize and acknowledge it. That is often more easily said than done, however, especially if people are afraid of anger and regard it as some sort of sin. If we cannot recognize it at once for what it is, we can at least recognize the physical manifestations (thumping heart, tightened throat, etc.) and the general feeling of unease. We do not make ourselves angry; it is an automatic response to a perceived threat that comes through our senses. We are not always responsible for being in a state of anger or for finding certain situations threatening. We are responsible for what we do with our anger. *Anger, in itself, is not sin, but anger misdirected can lead to great destructiveness, which is sin.* That is a different matter.

Blake's poem poses various crucial questions. Why could I tell my friend and not my foe? What constitutes the distinction between a friend and an enemy? How did I tell my friend? Did I just stand there and announce my anger with my friend, thinking that I was in the right and he was in the wrong, and then walk out leaving the basic issues unresolved? Was my intention solely to relieve my own tension? Was I simply deriving some dismal pleasure in my anger – a sort of justifiable resentment against a perceived wrong? Apparently not, because evidently my wrath disappeared and our relationship was restored. I wanted my friend to understand clearly what I was saying and feeling. I was interested in his response. I wanted to know how he was feeling and his point of view. My anger contained within it some space for restoration of the relationship, not simply condemnation and accusation.

It is not much good telling myself that I am not angry, if I actually am. We have to start from the place where we are, not from where we are not. Nor is it very helpful for me to tell myself that I ought not to be. That may be true, but it does little to help me to manage the anger constructively. That only pushes it under the carpet where it can continue its sinister activity. It is more helpful to enquire what all this anger is really about. If anger is usually a response to a perceived threat, what do I feel is being threatened? Is it my self-image, my position, my ambitions, a relationship or some other thing about which I feel very possessive? I begin to face the inner areas of neediness, frustration, fear, and unmet appetites within. Those are the things which make me become defensive and angry when I feel insecure. These areas may have been concealed carefully, from myself as well as other people, by a façade of competence, diligence, independence, overwork – or even saintliness. I have to face the fears that we have already discussed. I have to be prepared to be very honest about myself and how I feel, and search for the cause of this anger.

All this may be embarrassing and uncomfortable. I may not even be able to articulate the reasons for the anger, in which case I just have to stay with the feelings of discomfort until they reveal something to me. It is surprising how something will surface if I can wait for it. Obviously, if I have been trying to dodge my deep feelings all my life, they will not present themselves immediately just because my brain tells them to. But it is difficult to allow feelings of vague discomfort to hang around. It is so much easier to get rid of them by blaming the other person or by being rational ('It was just an off day') rather than waiting in openness and honesty.

We can regard our anger as having two levels of existence. At one level there are the obvious external outbursts of annoyance, irritation or temper. These are like the visible symptoms of a disease. At the other level is what we have been referring to as an infected blood stream or the cause of the symptoms. Both levels need attention. The external manifestations may need some soothing lotion but that alone is not enough. If we are really serious about getting to grips with our anger we have to go for the cause as well as for the effect. And the cause is almost always about not having an internal 'safe place' where we can go to rest confidently.

Another essential in the management of anger is to *share* that anger with a friend, if possible. That can sometimes be even more difficult than facing it myself unless I am at explosion point and full of Dutch courage. We put a severe limit on the value of telling our anger if telling it is our only concern. As we have seen already, ventilation of feelings, in itself, does not solve anything and can become addictive. We may be taking all sorts of risks by allowing other people to experience our anger. We may perhaps lose a friend if there is some real weakness in the relationship; we may lose our own self-image; we may go over the top a bit. We do take risks if we are ourselves and not a pale reflection of what we would like to think we are and what we want other people to see. That is the very reason why sharing our anger is so difficult. But unless we do take some risks we shall be imprisoned in our anger. We are only free to be angry with some degree of safety when there is a strong degree of trust.

We trust our friends but not our foes. We are not about to reveal our areas of vulnerability to them if we do not expect them to treat us with respect.

One obstacle to restoration of a relationship is the defensive position we may adopt. We could call it 'pride' but whatever its name, it is a refusal to admit that we may have misunderstood something or that we have been excessively needy or had any significant part in a difficult situation. To climb down in any way seems too much like admitting defeat. If a relationship of any quality is to continue, it is vital for both parties to be aware of and respect the feelings of the other, including the weaknesses, hurts and anger as well as the joys and love. In this way we grow as individuals and the relationship grows.

We have talked a lot about the importance of expressing our anger *con*structively and ways in which we can do it, but we have to remember that *de*struction is not always bad. For instance, I may decide that I would like a rosebed in my garden where at present there is a lawn. This means, inevitably, that I have to dig up the lawn and 'destroy' it. I can't have both. It is not 'bad' to dig up the lawn: it just means that if I want one thing I have to make room for it by changing something else. So it is with relationships: my anger may be indicating that I would prefer a different dynamic in the relationship, so I 'destroy' the one that is operating now in order to establish a better one. This is what Helen was doing in her diary in Chapter seven. Thus, if we want to express our anger constructively, there is bound to be an element of destruction.

We have to conclude that because we have all had frustrations, pain and anguish in the foundational years of life, our genetic inheritance and our early conditioning environment, we are all angry people: that is to say that we have this vital underground force flowing within. Some of us show it; some of us hide it – but basically, we are all prone to anger because we all have a child within us which stays with us all our life. Many people, alas, treat their inner child with considerable contempt as something inappropriate and foolish. That inner child has some of the penetrating wisdom of all children. It has a tremendous appreciation of mystery, and it has needy parts. Does it follow, then, that I am not *responsible* for my angry reactions in adulthood if someone provokes me? 'I can't help it,' we could say. 'That is the result of my experience and what I am.' We are not responsible for things over which we have no control but we are responsible for owning the anger in ourselves and not putting the blame somewhere else. Our responsibility lies in facing our own anger and its associated fears, pain or resentments.

But how can we get in touch with our inner anger if it is hidden away underneath layers of 'carpet' or 'niceness'? How are we to recognize it? Fortunately for us, anger is such a faithful ally that it does not usually lie quietly and poison us with no indication at all of what is happening. As we have seen in most of our case-studies there is usually some disturbing signal – a physical malfunction of some sort, emotional discomfort, or inability to form satisfying relationships – which alerts us to the fact that all is not well. The important thing, then, is to listen to what these symptoms are saying and not dismiss them with a bottle of alcohol or pills or 'pull yourself together and work it off'. Pills and work do help, of course, but not if they obscure the real underlying message.

Sometimes we need someone to help us to decipher the message because, by ourselves, we cannot see the wood for the trees. As we interpret these messages and absorb their meaning, we begin to get nearer and nearer to our true selves. Layers of 'niceness' or of defensiveness become unnecessary. We begin to see our wounding tongue, our intense busyness or even our intense spirituality, for example, in its true light – that is to say, as a way of avoiding facing ourselves. This is not morbid introspection, although it can become that if it does not help to free us from our defences and enable us to become more whole. It is a necessary part of our journey towards finding our true centre: being real. As we get nearer to our true selves, we have more of ourselves to enjoy, to give to God and to other people.

Christians often see their required response to anger in terms of a picture of St George slaying the dragon – the dragon being a fierce, angry beast which wreaks havoc everywhere so there is only one thing to do with it. The Christian task, they suppose, is to slay it so that it cannot rear its ugly head again. St George is the youthful knight in shining armour who plunges his spear into the monster which has no personal connection with him at all. There is a complete split between the two figures in the story; they operate from different focal points. This is not a true position for us. Anger is very much a personal thing and people are not pristine knights doing battle with anger. Anger is this most vital passion, familiar to God, and one of our most valuable personal assets. Anger itself is not sinful but it can be expressed in ways which are very destructive and wounding and that is what is sinful. It is also sinful to allow anger to go on simmering unresolved and unreconciled because it can become like a deadly cancer eating away at healthy flesh.

To change the metaphor completely, anger is like the accelerator in a car. When we are learning to drive, it has startling power, but when we become comfortable with total car management it is simply an extension of ourselves and can be used without anxiety or threat. Imagine what a car without an accelerator would be like! Only if we are immature and not quite at home with ourselves is it necessary to use the accelerator as a means of showing off or terrorizing people! (Incidentally, have you noticed that adults who are very inoffensive in everyday life can become lethally aggressive when they get behind the steering wheel and have access to the accelerator? Could the connection be something to do with inability to be angry in appropriate situations so the aggression comes out inappropriately?)

The constructive way of relating to anger is not to try to slay the dragon (or remove the accelerator) but to try to help it to find a home (or become integrated with the rest of the whole) so that it loses its ferocity, is more under control and becomes an ally rather than an enemy.

The Christian good news is that God's interest in us is not primarily to punish our sins and the anger which is within all of us. The good news is that we may experience his love. One result of this will be that our ability to be angry constructively will become a vibrant and purposeful part of living: not in flashes of temper but in direct achievement.

What is this *safe place* for a Christian? We were born into a world where anger is endemic, where its seeds are embedded in everybody by the inevitable nature of things. Even if we could enter a second time into our mother's womb and be born all over again for a second try, we would still have inner foundational frustrations, the faulty learning patterns and the genes to contend with. The safe place is described in 1 John 3.1: 'How great is the love the Father has lavished on us, that we should be called the children of God! *And that is what we are!*'

When Jesus Christ was on earth he demonstrated in his very first miracle how his coming touched precisely that very point. Jesus went to a wedding – a happy, normal, ordinary place to be: the place of human interaction, emotion, joy, perhaps some fear, leaving, joining, sometimes anger, sexuality and physicality. Then, amid the celebration the supply of wine was used up. No more for anyone. Jesus, aware of the need and embarrassing crisis, quietly told the servants to fill the stone water jars with water: six huge, empty jars each capable of holding between twenty and thirty gallons. They were in readiness for washing sticky hands and dusty feet. Jesus then told the servants to draw some of the water off and take it to the master of ceremonies. No fuss; no drama. It was the same ordinary water, but oh! how different. 'Why have you saved the best wine until now?' they said. He came to turn the water of our turbulent depths of human nature into the quality wine of spiritual life; not to throw it away and start something new, but to transform it. Spirituality is not something apart from the rest of our living. It includes our emotions and physicality. Water is one symbol of human life and many of Jesus' miracles are connected in some way with water. Jesus came to share our human life for the sole purpose of demonstrating God's love in a deeply personal way. When the inadequate and not-really-thirst-quenching water of our human life has been touched by Jesus it is transformed into a new level of experience: we are firmly rooted in our 'safe place'.

The Bible often uses water as a symbol. The prophet Ezekiel had an extraordinary vision about water flowing out of the temple in Jerusalem. At first the water was ankle deep; at the second point he was knee deep; at the third point he was waist deep; at the fourth point he could swim in it because it was too deep to be crossed on foot. This river then flowed down from Jerusalem into the valley where the river Jordan enters the Dead Sea. Perhaps some of us have a visual image of this sweltering scene: the blistering sun shining out of a hard, cloudless blue sky on the sea, 400 metres below sea level; the amber sunbaked mountains surrounding this great salt lake, offering no shade or protection to man or beast; no boats for fishing or for pleasure, because the extreme salt quality of the water would soon ruin them; no fish or plankton, because they could not live in that saline density; stumps of trees which have long since been petrified into unrecognizable shapes – and endless sweltering sun. Beautiful, in an arid, harsh sort of way. It is aptly called 'the Dead Sea'. Nothing will grow there, but nevertheless the water is rich in potential – thirty per cent minerals and very valuable.

In Ezekiel's vision he saw that when the river empties into the sea the water becomes fresh. Swarms of living creatures will live wherever the river flows because it makes the salt water fresh. Fishermen will stand along the shore; from En Gedi to En Eglaim there will be places for spreading nets. The fish will be of many kinds, like the fish of the Great (Mediterranean) Sea. (This picture is rather like a life touched by the love of God and consequently operating from a different source of spiritual awareness.) But the swamps and marshes will not become fresh; they will be left for salt. (Rather like bits of our original state which we still have to go on living with because although we are already redeemed we have not yet completed our redemption until we get to heaven.) Fruit trees of all kinds will grow on both banks of the river. Their leaves will not wither nor will their fruit fail. Every month they will bear, because the water from the sanctuary flows to them. Their fruit will be for food and their leaves for healing (Ezekiel 47.8–12).

This is an amazing picture! The transformation is unbelievable, but the sea (the person we knew before) is still identifiable as the same that the travellers know and visit. It has not changed its shape or location. Indeed, some of the salt remains. It is not totally destroyed and obliterated.

The Bible tells us that the first human beings were made by God in his own likeness in order that there could be a relationship between them. God breathed into this man the breath (spirit) of Life: not merely physical life but the capacity for spiritual awareness and intercourse with God as if speaking to a friend. That seems a bit mind-boggling because the world, on the whole, has lost both the desire and the capacity for it. We remain alive physically but dead on the level of Spirit (God's breath of life). So God took upon himself the likeness of human nature which he had made and came on earth at a precise point in historical time to restore the Life which had been lost. God's love was/is not an airy-fairy spirit of good-will. It was a costly business of redemption – buying back that which had been forfeited. We enjoy celebrating Christmas, but Easter was also in the plan. Without Christmas, Easter would be impossible, and without Easter (the death and resurrection), Christmas is meaningless: 'He too shared in their humanity so that by his death he might destroy him who holds the power of death – that is, the devil – and free those who all their lives were held in slavery by their fear of death' (Hebrews 2.14–15). Thus God's love makes it possible for us to be restored to a quality of life which has been lost; or to use the previous metaphor, possible for the dead sea to become alive.

Jesus had many conversations with people about this. He was saying constantly that he had come to restore mankind to its original purpose. 'On the last and greatest day of the Feast (one of the great annual celebrations of the Jews in Jerusalem) Jesus stood and said in a loud voice "If a man is thirsty, let him come to me and drink. Whoever believes in me, as the Scripture has said, streams of living water will flow from within him." By this he meant the Spirit ...' (John 7.37–8). Rivers of water, alive with Spirit, would flow out of inner self and their deep inner human nature, out of the people's seat of their anger, love, fear, sexuality and hunger.

This new truth is not about struggling to follow or imitate Christ, who is the Truth, or having him superimposed on me: it is about me being my own truth – alive with his Spirit, growing and developing within me over the years. It is about experiencing the 'living water' – a new quality of life which Jesus gives. This sounds like really good news! It has something relevant and healing to say about my deep inner frustrations, pain, hurt, and anger; about the hidden depths which may have become petrified through years of being malnourished and neglected.

This is the 'safe place' – the inner experience of the Spirit in among our earthiness and humanity. It is not about a split between the two. This is the place where our fragmentations, frustrations, appetites, needs and angers can be expressed, understood, met – and be made whole. It is not a case of reinforcing our defences against an internal struggle (employing a second Grace Poole, so to speak), but a change of orientation (a healing for Mrs Rochester and her re-entry into life). Our deep spiritual foundational needs are met, so that our human-spiritual nature is integrated. This is not magic. It is the costly love which we may receive as a gift. It is not something which can be grasped and understood in the mind however hard we try: it is something which we have to trust and commit ourselves to with the whole of our being and which we will only come to know as we do it. Then we shall have been born of flesh and spirit – both!

Self-control is one of those fruits that grow on the trees beside the river that flows into our dead sea. The influx of this life-giving water does not mean that we shall never be angry again. Far from it. It means that we gain courage to be firm and angry when necessary, to confront or draw limits without experiencing crippling fear. It means that our anger is much more likely to be constructive because there is no hidden agenda of self-protection. It also means that we can be on the receiving end of other people's anger without the need to hit back in some ill-judged way. We do not need to feel threatened. It does not mean that we do not experience the anger but it does mean that we can contain it without an undifferentiated explosion; or perhaps we can deflect it by a gentle answer which does not contain a sting. Self-control does not mean stifling our anger or pretending it does not exist. That is recipe for trouble.

As we said in Chapter four, we sometimes confuse ourselves by quoting, out of context, sayings like 'not I, but Christ', as though the 'I' in me must be crossed out and cease to function and have the 'Christ' superimposed on it. So what happens to the 'I'? We all know that it does not cease to function. Are we supposed to beat it into submission somehow, with varying degrees of success or failure and not much genuine joy? Or is 'Christ' banished to the sidelines and kept for Sundays and special occasions? Here is a dilemma. In either case a part of us is split off and in conflict with the rest. We are trying to operate from two different focal points at the same time – which is a hopeless impossibility.

No, thank God, this is not the message! The message is about the river of life coming in to transform my personal Dead Sea, which has great value, but where nothing much can live without the fresh water.

If we are thinking of the resolution of anger and hurt, we must encounter the issue of *forgiveness*. Where there is willingness to forgive – and forget (i.e. not to hold a secret grudge, and not to have the thing hidden away under the carpet out of sight but not out of mind) – there can be resolution.

Someone says or does something which we find deeply wounding. There may be some element of truth which is hard for us to accept or the things said or done may be totally unwarranted. Either way, our inner spirit has been offended and distressed. Forgiveness, if it means anything, is usually costly. I have been deeply hurt and I cannot just sweep it away with vague words about 'one of those things' or 'the love of God'. Nor am I required to think that it must be all my fault and I must take the blame for everything. I may be under the impression that because a feeling of discomfort exists, that in itself is 'wrong' and must be got rid of, so I must 'forgive' as soon as possible in order that the unpleasant feelings may go away. Forgiveness is not primarily about getting rid of unpleasant feelings: it is about restoring and deepening relationships. The hurt and anger has to be faced. What has been hurt? Is it my self-esteem, which may be fragile and cannot take knocks like this? Is it my love which has been trampled on so painfully? Is it some blatant injustice or lack of recognition or some misrepresentation of the truth?

Then I am faced with an almost conscious decision. Do I want to perpetuate this feeling of outrage – regardless of how justified, or not, it seems? If not, am I prepared to let go of it? If the hurt has been very deep, I may be involved in a struggle of mammoth proportions while I relinquish my 'rights' or while I engage in a different way with the person whose love seems to be so essential. Forgiveness is not cheap. It may take me to the roots of my being and may require time.

I may have reached a point where I am willing to acknowledge the offence and forgive, but that may be as far as it is possible to go. If the other person does not ask for forgiveness, I may have to stop there, with regret. But my forgiving attitude will inevitably make some difference to the dynamic of the relationship.

Suppose I have been the person who caused the offence and did those hurtful and anger-producing things. I am then faced with the same issues. What was all this about? Did I think I was being threatened – overtly or silently? What was being threatened? Was it my self-esteem, when the chips are down? Could I have responded differently and if so, what stopped me? Am I truly sorry, not because the ensuing fuss may have shown me up in a bad light, but because I have caused distress to someone, whether I realized it or not? And then, perhaps the hardest part of all, I have to go and tell them that I am sorry and, if possible, make restitution. Be angry and do not sin: do not let the sun go down on your anger!

A powerful jolt comes as we recite the Lord's Prayer and ask '... forgive us our sins as we forgive those who sin against us ... .' Can we expect God's forgiveness if we are not prepared to forgive our fellow-sinners? I was in church at a Communion service the other day and a man behind me was articulating the General Confession with great confidence: 'We acknowledge and bewail our manifold sins and wickedness which we from time to time most grievously have committed by thought, word and deed, against thy divine majesty, provoking most justly thy wrath and indignation against us ...' he announced. I happened to know that this man was in the middle of particularly messy divorce proceedings causing hurt and distress to all concerned. He considered himself to be the innocent party, of course. And I caught myself thinking 'At the very least he might moderate his voice a little!' And then I remembered the 'he who is angry at another man's faults and is not angry at his own is a hypocrite'!

Willingness to forgive is at the heart of Christian experience. It was when Jesus was on the receiving end of anger, violence and the most unjust bigotry that he said 'Father, forgive them ... .' Forgiveness is not the inability to cope with anger. On the contrary, it is exactly the reverse.

A newborn baby has physical life and an old man has physical life. Both have life, but one has years of maturity and experience. So with the flesh-spirit life: there is a constant process of growth, familiarity and change. There is also the constant vigilance about keeping the watercourses clean and unblocked, and sometimes this involves battling and struggling against would-be encroachments.

And so it continues until we leave the troubles and sorrows of this mortal life and discover the true extent of the life for which we were originally created.

The mess of anger (or other messy feelings) is not something to be cleared up. It is rather to be understood in the whole package of what makes me the person I am. The peace achieved by pushing a disturbance under the carpet is not the same as the peace of integration.

Chapter eleven

Holy wrath

The anger of God is hard to understand and theologians down the centuries have been trying to grapple with it. In the Old Testament we read horrendous accounts of wholesale slaughter, plague, storm and pestilence as a result of God's being angry with the nations. Individuals, too, have dire punishments meted out to them and some may seem to us to be excessive and incomprehensible. God's anger is not a popular subject these days. We hear a great deal about the love of God, but as we saw earlier, love and anger are two sides of one coin – inseparable. So we need to take God's anger seriously. We would rather not: we know from our own experience how frightening anger can be, both in ourselves and in other people. When we associate the ideas of both an all-powerful and an angry God, it becomes truly terrifying. One good way of defending ourselves against this terror is to deny the reality of God's anger. If we don't look at it, it might go away. Or we could tell ourselves that this is a projection of our own bad feelings. We are too sophisticated and civilized, these days, to believe in such primitive ideas as an angry god; and so we dismiss the idea and leave it unresolved.

When we look at the examples of God's anger in the Bible we often find that, somewhere in the account, God says the phrase 'I AM the Lord: that is my name'. We know that in those days a person's name was intended to give some indication of his character. So in his anger, God was reminding the people that he was holy, strong, faithful and that his righteous nature would not change. He was outraged that his image was defaced, that consequently, people were defacing themselves, and that the earth generally was being despoiled. (A faint echo of this may be when we see graffiti scrawled all over public transport and walls.) He was also saying that his strong love could not be watered down into 'turning a blind eye' or pretending that violations of his character did not matter. That would have been cheap forgiveness. Alastair Campbell, in *The Gospel of Anger*, suggests that 'perhaps the dark shadow of destructive aggression emanating from divine wrath is just our limited view of the brilliance of divine love'.[1] And T. S. Eliot, in *Little Gidding*, says:

> *Who then devised the torment? Love.*
> *Love is the unfamiliar Name*
> *Behind the hands that wove*
> *The intolerable shirt of flame*
> *Which human power cannot remove'.*[2]

It is as though his anger is 'God's strange work' (Isaiah 28.21). 'Strange' in the sense of 'alien'. His natural, 'proper' work is grace and compassion in love. When people repent and change their deep attitudes and consequent behaviour, God always relents and is merciful. It would be unrighteous to continue with anger in the face of repentance. Both the strange and the proper work are necessary in the task of enabling us to grow in the knowledge of God. We cannot have one without the other. Without the knowledge of his anger, we come to see God as some sort of celestial Santa Claus whom we regard with fond contempt. We expect him to hand out the goodies from time to time but do not believe he is really there. God's anger and love are in essential balance with one another.

There are some situations where injustice and outrageous inhumanity arouse our righteous anger. These are some of the occasions when passionate protest may lead to action which produces results. There are many social issues about which vigorous protest needs to be made. We need such anger and should show more of it, but many of us are content with passive anger. Our love needs to be strong enough to allow us to be vigorously angry. Our lack of such anger is a sin of omission, as much to be condemned as sins of commission. The unequal distribution of the world's wealth, the wanton destruction of our planet, the plight of the starving and the physical or emotional abuse of children and refugees, are obvious causes of outrage.

Some issues, without doubt, should make us *righteously angry*; but the righteous quality of our anger is not quite the same thing. It is true that we have to be strong to make our loving effective, but it is very hard to be sure that there is no self-interest at all attached to our anger; or that we may be protesting verbally but are unprepared to alter our lifestyle to back up our protest. During the Gulf War with all its complex issues we were properly angry against aggression and cruelty to innocent people; but at the same time we had to remember that God is angry with us all for the perversion of our intelligence in devising various obscene weapons of war with all the devastation that they can bring, and our love of an easy lifestyle. If the money spent on weapons on the first day of 'Desert Storm' had been spent in Africa, there need not be one starving person there. I am told that a few years ago, when women were protesting against the nuclear weapons base at Greenham Common, a group of outraged, respectable, middle-class residents from a nearby town visited the women's unsalubrious camp one night and poured bottles of blood and maggots into their tents. It seems incredible, but we are left to assume that the visitors were pouring out all the bottled up venom inside themselves against the women who were 'spoiling their countryside'. Whatever else they did, the women uncovered the rottenness and destruction hidden away in the hearts of 'respectable' townspeople.

We have seen groups of people split apart by what goes under the name of 'righteous anger' or 'defence of the truth'. One group may perceive that some practice or doctrine that they hold very dear is being threatened by something less 'pure' and they go all out in defence of it. Here again, we meet the familiar scenario of anger being the response to threat – and sometimes the anger can be very destructive. Would that we listened more often to the advice of Gamaliel, the celebrated teacher among Jews! When Peter and the other apostles had been preaching in Jerusalem about the Jesus who had been crucified there so recently, the high priest and his associates 'were furious and wanted to put them to death ... But Gamaliel ... stood up ... and said ... "Leave these men alone! Let them go! For if their purpose is of human origin, it will fail. But if it is from God, you will not be able to stop these men. You will only find yourselves fighting against God"' (Acts 5.33–9).

We have to be somewhat careful about righteous anger.

Conclusion

So we have come to the end of our journey round the edges of anger. It is one thing to read about anger; it is quite another to experience it. As it becomes a living experience, it is transformed into something else. It is the stuff of life! Anger is usually against some person and what they have done. It is vital that we engage in some way with both the anger and the person if the anger is to be transformed. Everything depends on acknowledging the anger and the way in which we engage with it.

Anger is of basic importance to our human life. It is often at the root of our motivations, lifestyle and relationships and so it frequently determines the sort of people we are. It is an essential part of health because it is potentially life-preserving.

It comes in many guises and the more we are afraid of it, the greater its number of disguises. It is such a powerful emotion that it can cause devastation if it is not understood and handled appropriately. Because of its power and its potentially traumatic effects, many people do their best to avoid it, often using a 'Christian' rationale for so doing. We are seduced into avoiding anger rather than facing it in the vain hope that we shall thereby minimize the trauma. But if we are to maximize the potential for growth and change, anger has to be acknowledged, called by its proper name and engaged with appropriately.

In his *Way of the Heart* Henri Nouwen says:

What else is anger but the impulsive response to the

experience of being deprived? When my sense of self depends on what others say of me, anger is a quite natural reaction to a critical word... . Anger in particular seems close to a professional vice in the contemporary ministry ... not an open, blatant, roaring anger, but an anger hidden behind the smooth word, the smiling face and the polite handshake. It is a frozen anger, an anger which settles into biting resentment and slowly paralyses a generous heart. If there is anything that makes the (Christian) ministry look grim and dull, it is this dark, insidious anger in the servants of Christ.[1]

The seeds of anger lie within us all. They come from the frustrations which are part of the world into which we have been born. Our earliest experiences in childhood determine gut-level satisfaction or frustration which will characterize our subsequent ability to tolerate frustration in adult life. One of our basic human needs is acceptance and love. This is essential in establishing a healthy self-esteem; without it we are at risk emotionally, are easily threatened and thrown off balance. The defence against this is anger, which is designed to keep the 'enemy' at bay, but which may in fact reveal our own vulnerability.

Later in life we may encounter a relationship of love within which some of the earlier wounds have an opportunity to be healed; within marriage, perhaps, or a close friendship, or maybe even through some formal therapeutic relationship. God uses these means as well as direct contact with himself to help us to find our true self. Layers of defensive protection gradually drop away and we come nearer to our heart that we have never known fully before. Then there is no need to be constantly aggressive or afraid. We shall be able to see this valuable asset for what it is.

There is a great difference between the experience of losing one's temper and being angry. They are not at all the same thing. When we 'flip our lid', 'go mad', or whatever we call it, and flail about in all directions, we are at the mercy of our driving anger. The dam has broken suddenly, and the surrounding land has become flooded, animals are washed away and houses ruined. People wade around trying to salvage what is left. Such are the results of losing one's temper. It is a kind of 'Mrs Rochester' experience. She is trying to say something valid but she does it in such a way that she leaves everyone battered and terrified and even more determined to strengthen the locks and bars and not hear her. But she has to express herself in this alarming way precisely because she cannot make herself heard in any other way. Perhaps the only good thing about loss of temper is that then the uninhibited truth comes out and we say what we really mean, however much we may try to backtrack afterwards. It certainly gives a clear message that something is very wrong. These awful scenes are usually physically and emotionally exhausting for all concerned. They are evidence of extreme and undealt-with frustration. Sometimes they produce results by themselves but they seldom improve relationships.

Being angry, on the other hand, is like following a river through the countryside. The driving force is sometimes still and tranquil, sometimes wide and fast, and sometimes a roaring torrent, but always flowing within its banks. It can be harnessed to irrigate the surrounding countryside. It is source of life and interest. It is not a threat, unless the banks are unsafe. It is a source of power.

There is an incident in *The Warden*, the first of Anthony Trollope's *Barchester Chronicles*, where the archdeacon is fulminating in explosive fury against the assertion that the Hiram's Hospital funds are not being administered properly.

The warden, Mr Harding, received £400 per year and the inmates only 1/8d. per day. Mr Harding himself was deeply hurt and angry about this unjust allegation. He turned it all over in his mind, played his feelings on his cello and lived his anger quietly until, eventually, he emerged with his customary serenity. The bishop's comment about him was: 'Mr Harding suffers from persistent bouts of Christianity.'

Anger is a basic motivating force in our life. How we use it or how it uses us is the crucial question.

Epilogue

With great hesitation, I tell you a personal story, though some things are difficult to put into words.

I have just been doing some sorting out, and wading through one of those huge boxes of photographs that one accumulates over the years. I found myself gazing at and pondering over sundry photographs of my immediate family, and smiling over the changes that have taken place in fashions. I went with each person, individually, into some of the surprises, joys and deep sorrows that were awaiting them, all unexpectedly. I looked at my parents; dear, good people who provided me with such a solid background; and my siblings and the loves and hates that were ranged around. We stood there, posing like every other family does, looking like a normal collection of people, which we were. But the camera cannot capture the family inter-relationships.

The person who mainly captured my attention on this occasion, was my mother: that lady who did her best for me and found me so impossible to manage. She saw to it that I was fed, clothed, educated and became reasonably civilized, and she was always there when I came home from school. She gave me every assistance that she could – except her 'presence'. I never remember sitting on her knee (though I am sure I did) nor of her telling me that she loved me (which she undoubtedly did). I do remember many scoldings and much disgrace and a very scratchy relationship between us. I would not have dreamt of telling her my little girl secrets: they were for the dog. I soon learnt, in that family, that being small, dependent and vulnerable was not acceptable. The important thing was to grow up as quickly as possible and stop being stupid and childish. I was not a very docile person and there were many uproars about this and that, so I learnt that anger was certainly not acceptable and did not pay. Its consequences were too unpleasant and dangerous.

So I grew up, having absorbed the idea that I must be competent, strong and able to manage my own affairs. Weakness and vulnerability were to be avoided at all costs because they were 'childish'. I had also collected the impression that I had to be a 'victorious Christian', which seemed to mean that I was not to be subject, from time to time, to normal human feelings. If they were joyful, that was acceptable; but if they smacked of discomfort in any way they were to be strangled at birth. I had the idea that self-denial meant wearing an emotional hair shirt and being harsh and unsympathetic with myself.

Thus, I struggled with life and the Christian way, full of good works and subject to generalized depression, often feeling negative and having a problem with prayer. I was able to sweep most of this under the carpet by having such a busy life that there wasn't any opportunity to look deeply at the spectre that I was vaguely aware lay below the surface. Once or twice I had a quite severe stress-induced illness but quickly soldiered back to the front line again. At the same time, I had lots of friends, lots of fun and lots of good things which acted as a very effective smoke screen.

At a certain point, I was driven by an inner sense that some things within were very wrong and I did not know how to sort them out in spite of much prayer and effort. I summoned every ounce of courage and decided to engage in a period of Jungian analysis. (It was easy for me to relate to other people who needed help but to admit that I needed anything was a very different kettle of fish. That was too much like being childish and stupid.) During that period of analysis I went with my analytic 'mother' into some of those black patches of no 'presence', of murderous rage (hiteerto denied) and terrible rejection. It was a long, hard and very painful struggle.

But gradually things changed. It was like watching the dawn break and the world silently becoming suffused with light. I began to experience in a new way which words cannot convey, that the personal 'presence' was always there, through the good times and the times of unpleasantness, of anger, of boredom. If I adopted the 'withdrawal' stance, or was trying to control everything myself, or was too hurt to recognize the underlying anger, I put myself outside the warmth of the sustaining presence. Slowly, I experienced that it was safe to be small and vulnerable and dependent at times, and then I began to experience that in a childlike way I could actually ask for and accept the tenderness that I needed from my mother (and my inner self). This soon extended to other people and to God. Again, just like the dawn, it 'happened' without any noise or great flash of lightning. I began to have the sense of wanting to be with God prayerfully, of knowing in my heart that he wanted me to be there and to care for me; of being in his presence like a little loved child – not knowing much, not being able to control anything, but just trusting. A new sort of trust. Previously I had been trying hard to believe with my brain something I did not experience in my heart as true. Now I understood that faith is not a cerebral matter: it is an experience of the heart. A gentle sense of quiet joy seemed to come with that trust: it felt as though many years of burdensome, rumbling anger had melted away in the sunshine of the 'presence'. I know that does not mean that life henceforth will be one long rosy dream. But I hope that I shall be more able to grieve the losses, and face the pains, angers and difficulties that may come, because of experiencing in a new way the 'presence of God' – the living water.

My experience is special to me, of course, but I add it because I think, deep down, it is really fairly typical of many people.

I have on my mantlepiece a little card bearing these words:

The Lord will give
Beauty for ashes,
Joy instead of mourning,
A garment of praise
Instead of a spirit of despair.   (Isaiah 61.3)

Notes

Chapter one
1. All biblical quotations are from the *Holy Bible, New International Version*, Copyright © 1973, 1978, 1984 by International Bible Society. Used by permission of Hodder and Stoughton Ltd.

Chapter two
1. A N Wilson: *C S Lewis* (Collins 1990)
2. Marjorie Thompson: *The Velveteen Rabbit* (Heinemann 1970)

Chapter four
1. Stephen Verney: *Water into Wine* (Fount Paperbacks 1985)

Chapter five
1. Susan Howatch: *Ultimate Prizes* (Collins 1989)

Chapter eight
1. Christina Rossetti (1830–94)
2. Charlotte Brontë (1816–55)

Chapter nine
1. Rosamunde Pilcher: *The Shell Seekers* (New English Library 1987)
2. C S Lewis: *A Grief Observed* (Faber and Faber 1961)

Chapter ten
1. William Blake (1757–1827)

Chapter eleven
1. Alastair Campbell: *The Gospel of Anger* (SPCK 1966)
2. T S Eliot: *Collected Poems* 1909–1962 (Faber and Faber 1963)

Conclusion
1. Henri Nouwen: *Way of the Heart* (DLT Daybreak 1990)

Suggested further reading

Alistair Campbell, *The Gospel of Anger* (SPCK 1986)

Myra Chave-Jones, *Coping With Depression* (Lion 1981)

Myra Chave-Jones, *Listening to Your Feelings* (Lion 1989)

Harold S Kushner, *When Bad Things Happen to Good People* (Pan 1982)

Gordon MacDonald, *Magnificent Marriage* (Scripture Press 1990)

Robin Skynner and John Cleese, *Families and How to Survive Them* (Mandarin/Methuen 1983)

Anthony Storr, *Human Aggression* (Penguin 1971)

Stephen Verney, *Water into Wine* (Fount 1985)

D W Winnicott, *The Child, the Family and the Outside World* (Pelican 1964)

Also published by

TRİ∆NGLE

HOW MANY TIMES CAN YOU SAY GOODBYE?
Living with bereavement
by Jenifer Pardoe

A down-to-earth look at grief, with many everyday stories to give practical insights into what can be done to understand and help in times of bereavement.

LOSING AND LIVING
Thoughts on every kind of grieving
by David M Owen

Considers a range of personal losses – from bereavement of family and friends in death to the loss of our own health, youth or job. It includes many apt and revealing quotations which speak directly of the experience of grief.

SEVEN FOR A SECRET THAT'S NEVER BEEN TOLD
Healing the wounds of sexual abuse in childhood
by Tracy Hansen

A moving account of a survivor of child sexual abuse working through the trauma induced by the return of repressed memories.

UNWORLD PEOPLE
For anyone who has felt unwanted, unusable, unloved
by Joyce Landorf Heatherley

Shows the growth of hope and faith after rejection, based on the author's own experience.

LIFE LATER ON
Older people and the church
by Ann Webber

A look at what Christians have to offer older people and vice versa.

FROM WHERE I SIT
Living with disability in an able-bodied world
by Alison Davis

A disturbing, personal and often funny account of what it is really like to be disabled.

WHO'S THIS SITTING IN MY PEW?
Mentally handicapped people in the church
by Faith Bowers

Considers what the church can do for mentally handicapped people and what they bring to the church.

TRI/\NGlE
Books
can be obtained from
all good bookshops.
In case of difficulty,
or for a complete list of our books,
contact:
SPCK Mail Order
36 Steep Hill
Lincoln
LN2 1LU
(tel: 0522 527 486)